Loving in Fear

Lesbian and Gay Survivors of Childhood Sexual Abuse

Edited by the Queer Press Collective

Canadian Cataloguing in Publication Data

Main entry under title:
Loving in Fear

ISBN 1-895564-00-X

1. Adult child sexual abuse victims — Literary collections.
2. Lesbians — Literary collections.
3. Gay men — Literary collections.
4. Lesbians' writings, Canadian (English).*
5. Gays' writings, Canadian (English).*
6. Homosexuality - Literary collections.

PS8235.L4L6 1991 C810.8'0353 C91-095688-X
PR9194.5.L4L6 1991

Cover design and artwork by Martha Newbigging

Published by
Queer Press Non-Profit Community Publishing of Toronto
P.O. Box 485 Station P Toronto, Ontario M5S 2T1

Contents

Just Listen
Inga-Britt 11
these cuts and scrapes
ki namaste 14
Family Secrets
Lorna Boschman 15
Joe/Rape Poem
Karen Augustine 19
bap/tis/him
Valerie Cain 22
Choices
Richard Hofmann 23
Red Running Shoes
Jean Noble 28
Pages 202–203
Louise Karch 43
Putting on a Happy Face
Louise Karch 45
Facing the Aftermath
Charles 48
Crooked Man
Sapphire 52
Ten Minute Salvation
Z. Love 55
Boxing Days: A Story
Rick Hammond 57
Killer Bees
Valerie Laub 75

The Shield
Valerie Laub 76
I Have No Name
Stevi Urben 78
Daddy is going to make you feel good
Stefan 79
Don't Touch Me
Whyte Ravyn 82
The Little Things
Whyte Ravyn 83
Timesharing
Whyte Ravyn 84
The Basement
Sophia Kelly 88
Stand Up and Be Discounted
David John 90
Sex at Six
Charlene Williams 95
Sexual Abuse by Both Genders
Becca 98
My Story
Steven Gauvin 102
Picnic
Laura Ardiel 106
Dead Wolf
Andrew Griffin 108
Breaking the Silence
Rhonda Hackett 111

What Dread Hand?
John David Pastway 114
Multiple Personality
Regan McClure 117
Exploring Legal Options
Carol Allen 128
Identifying Your
Own Healing Path
Clarissa Chandler 144

Contributors' Notes 153

Acknowledgments

We never would have guessed how many people it actually takes to put together a book. Everyone who put up a poster, became a member, took a shift at the computer, or dropped some change into our donation jar, we thank you — every bit of help contributed to this final product. The Queer Press Collective, consisting of Regan McClure, Lynn Iding and Shenaz Stri, would especially like to thank the following people:

Anne Vespry, for her inspiration in starting the press, Milagros Paredes for allowing us to use the title, Women's Press (especially Heather), Gynergy, and Sister Vision Press for showing us how it all works, Nola Coulter and Faith By-the-well for help in the selection process, The Women's Centre at the University of Toronto, Andrea Calver for hours of proofreading, and the Lesbian and Gay Community Appeal and the John Damian Educational Trust for financial support.

Several people helped to advertise, distribute flyers, and worked at our fundraisers. Although this list is by no means complete, we would like to express our appreciation to Sue Reynolds, Michael Armstrong, Faith By-the-well, Caireen Ryan (hamburger flipper extrordinaire), Livia Resendes, Terry Nelson and Nola Coulter. A big thank you also goes to Burger, and the staff at the 457.

On the more personal side, where would this frazzled collective be without the support and inspiration from the people we care about. Regan would like to thank Rhonda "for believing my scribbled notes, and for ongoing spiritual, emotional, and financial support" and Lynn thanks Livia "for listening to me whine and complain, and for always being my best buddy," and Tsigane, "wherever you are". Shenaz would like to thank Sylvana and Margaret for their support.

Introduction

Queer Press Non-Profit Community Publishing of Toronto, also known as Queer Press, was started by and for lesbians and gay men to publish the work of queer authors, poets, playwrights and artists. We are committed to supporting the work of those who have historically been marginalized, as well as to publishing a balance of work by both lesbians and gay men. We also donate three percent of all the books we publish to queers in prisons and psychiatric institutions. *Loving in Fear,* Queer Press' first publication, was made possible in large part by the many people who donated time and money, or who became members. A lifetime membership to the press is available for twenty five dollars, and will entitle you to a twenty percent discount on everything we publish, and will get you on our mailing list. We will continue to appreciate and rely on your support for future Queer Press publications.

The response to this anthology was quite overwhelming. We received many contributions from lesbians and gays from a wide diversity of backgrounds and experiences. Using poetry, prose, and analytical essays, the writers told their stories, and linked the violence of childhood sexual abuse to the hatred and oppression of homophobia we all experience as queers.

Each one of us is loving in fear when we drop the hand of a lover in public places, or when we uncomfortably avoid the question "Are you married?", just as a survivor shudders at the echoes of old memories when touched in a certain way. We love in fear when we stay away from children, knowing what 'they' say about queers, or when desperately wanting to shower after receiving a hug and enjoying it. We are loving in fear when we face the hostility towards us as we come out as queers, as feminists, as survivors of sexual, emotional, physical and ritual abuse, or as queers fighting against racist and economic oppression.

We are all meant to be loving in fear — kept in our place by the lies and myths surrounding our existence. The people who tell us that abuse is the cause of being queer — now that the problem is identified they can work to fix us — or say that queers are all perpetrators of abuse, want to keep us loving in fear. But we struggle; we resist. We may be afraid, but we are still surviving, still organizing and still loving each other and ourselves. Our loving is an act of revolution — knowing that our voices and our truths will certainly disrupt the 'natural' social order, which has kept us silenced and invisible for so long.

Whenever we break the silence, as survivors, lovers, friends, and as queers, we are fighting for the right to love as we choose.

The Queer Press Collective

Just Listen

Inga-Britt

1. I'm 8 — he's 14
He has an affair — with me
I'll remember 12 years later.

2. I'm 19 — another brother (24)
His tongue in my mouth
His hands all over me
Never forgot that.

3. Don't know how old
I don't know what
He was father
alcoholic, angry, not there
I want to / don't want to
remember
Some day I'll know.

4. Don't know who, when, why
His penis was in my mouth
Maybe I'll never know
Yet it is reality — oral rape.

5. I'm 1
Mother is washing me
green bucket — in kitchen
Who else was there?
Extreme attention for
my genitals
She rubs and rubs and rubs ...

I'm 5
Nothing is different
They've built an addition to house
We've got separate bathroom
Now I'm bathing with
4 1/2 year older brother
Hardly surprising I forgot.

6. I'm 20
I start remembering my life
surfacing with power
pain, panic, fear.

7. I'm woman
I love women
spirit, attraction, love
I — WOMAN.

8. Don't say: You're lesbian because...
Don't. Just don't.
Don't assume that there's
something wrong with being lesbian
with loving
with loving women.

9. Don't suggest that
they aren't quite responsible
They didn't have to abuse me
INCEST
They've had other choices
I — VICTIM

10. Don't ask: Is it possible?
That you're a lesbian because
your mother abused you?
Don't. Just don't.

My father, my brothers,
they abused me too, sexually
You don't make any sense, you
who says so, asks so.
No trauma 'makes' someone
homosexual.
I'm not a lesbian because of...
I'm not a lesbian in spite of...
I am lesbian.
It is that simple:
I am lesbian because I am lesbian.
I am INCEST SURVIVOR
I am LESBIAN
I am WOMAN
I am.
Alive.

these cuts and scrapes

ki namaste

" How did you hurt your eye, son?"
(i was raped)

" Let me get you some gauze..."
(your husband did it to me)

" How did you cut your lip?"
(he told me to shut up and bit me savagely)

" Let me fetch some ointment..."
(i told him " no" — i begged, i pleaded, i screamed)

" Did you fall and bruise your arms?"
(he pinned me with such force, i was helpless)

" Oh, I see you have a rug burn..."
(he dragged me across the room, told me i was worthless)

" Gee, it must have been quite a tumble..."
(he used his penis like a bludgeon)

" Was it down a flight of stairs?"
(he ripped my insides open)

" Well, you'll be better soon"
(i haven't stopped bleeding yet)

" These cuts and scrapes heal quickly you know"
(i will never be the same)

" Why are you so quiet, child?"
(i [am young therefore i] am silenced)

Family Secrets

Lorna Boschman

It has been almost two years since I began to remember what I always knew was missing.

In 1988, I was working on three separate projects dealing with sex — two weeks of performance, media and installation celebrating female sexuality, a lesbian erotic film and a video conversation between myself and Jean B. where we talked about our childhoods. Jean was sexually abused, and I said I was 'only' physically and emotionally abused. At this time, I thought I'd had a more 'normal' childhood.

While we were taping this video, Jean, who knew me pretty well, kept asking if I had ever been sexually abused. "No way!", I said. "But if anyone had been abusing you, who would it have been?" she asked. "My grandfather," I said. Of course, I edited that section out of the video.

Making that video turned me into a crabby person. I had always been fairly even tempered, but this video just set me off. I walked around in a rage most of the time, waiting for someone to say the wrong thing so I could attack them.

I kept wondering why talking about physical abuse, which I had always remembered, had started to upset me like that.

Editing this video was harder than shooting it. We shot it in two days, but the editing dragged on for months. I wanted the material to come from the child's point of view, to say for us what we had been denied by our parents. Somehow, by stating our memories in public, we felt we would have a better chance of being believed. But the child who is being abused is told that they cannot tell, or bad things will happen. I wanted to speak out, but feared the consequences. It was a conflict that went on for months while I edited. And I was actively trying not to remember that I had been sexually abused as a child. It's no wonder I was a crabby person.

At the suggestion of a friend, I started homeopathic treatments, which finally pushed me over the edge. One night, while having sex, I got so upset that my girlfriend forced me to talk about it. When she asked me what my feelings reminded me of, I told her about this time I went fishing with my grandfather. The scene was so vibrant, the colours so brilliant, I was only three years old and my grandfather was masturbating while I watched him. He put my hand on his penis. When I got home, I told my mother that he had brought a sausage with us in the boat, and she beat me for being a liar.

That was just the first of many memories. While I was remembering all of this, I felt like my skin was crawling. But I didn't want to give up on sex just because it made me think of disembodied penises. Whenever I had sex, I was disoriented for days. First, I would just feel dirty, and then I'd want to kill myself. My closest call was almost being hit by a train. Always look both ways before crossing the tracks! I called my new personality 'Brutella the Hun' because I was constantly in a rage. I remembered a dozen sexual encounters between myself and my grandfather which happened before I turned six.

I was my grandfather's favourite, and no one could understand why, since the guy hated children. We would go walking, fishing...I thought I was a boy and he was my teacher.

When I was fourteen, he was dying of lung cancer. My parents had to force me to go there, to see him before he died. "Why would I want to see him?" Then they told me that I was his favourite, that he had been asking for me. It didn't make much sense to me — I couldn't even remember him, or anything else that far back.

When I mention going through this "incest stuff", people ask me who my therapist is. I'll admit that my lover is an experienced peer counsellor, and that we talk about our emotions with each other. But after a few bad experiences years ago, I gave up on 'feminist' or any other form of therapy. I guess I can't follow the modern religion.

I knew that I wanted to use the materials from my memories in my work as a media artist. My hesitation about therapy sprang from a fear that I'd become addicted to the jargon of therapy or otherwise indoctrinated in the use of that language. But it's not just the jargon that bothered me. Therapy picks through your experiences, gives them a category and tells you how to feel about them. It's as if all of our unique individual experiences can be collapsed into one category: incest survivor. I wanted my experiences to be in my art and to be fresh and immediate, not a reworking of someone else's interpretation.

I have plenty of friends for whom therapy works, but it is not for me. Sometimes, I think my cultural background as a Mennonite orients me toward the direct experience, without benefit of an intermediary. Or maybe the result of abuse is that I don't trust strangers with private information unless I control it through my work. In moments of self-doubt, I wonder if my emotional suffering would be over with faster if I did attend therapy. But I stubbornly hope for salvation through artistic procreation.

When I feel particularly down, I wonder if this will go on forever: this anger, the fear, this sensitivity to innocent (?) flirtation, this general confusion about sex. When people are too affectionate, I wonder if they are coming on to me. Is it my imagination, or is sex part of most relationships, even if it's not overt? Maybe I would not have remembered my abuse if I hadn't been in a long-term, stable and supportive relationship. Maybe I wouldn't have noticed, if my artistic style was not to expose myself, to exploit my vulnerabilities for the benefit of my work.

Remembering the incest memories has caused a sexual identity crisis. Not about being a lesbian, since I have always been one, but about sex itself. Pursuit of sex had been a major part of my life — to be wild, have lots of lovers, to prove that, in spite of my faults, I was desirable. Now, I actually prefer work over another affair. Have I become settled down with my lover and my dog, non-monogamous in name alone? I still feel attracted to other women, but something stops me from having sex with them. Maybe it is because being fucked while remembering incest is emotionally too dangerous. The wrong move, or even the right one, can send me back emotionally to a time when I was little and there was nothing I could do to prevent another sexual encounter. I guess it has something to do with trust.

After a year of remembering, I decided to use the material from my first memory in a film. It was so visually stunning in my mind that I wanted to show it off. Kim Blain and I worked on the script for a film on incest. The concept of the film is to show an innocent scenario — a grandfather and child fishing on a lake. From the outside, the picture is idyllic and calm. But inside, where no one can really see it, the reality of the scene takes place. The viewer sees beautiful image of the two, reflected on a totally calm lake. On the soundtrack, the grandfather is seducing the child: "Such a pretty girl, you're pretty you know, just like a fairy princess..."

After cutting the grandfather's dialogue for that scene, I went into shock. Kim was out running an errand while I tried to match picture and sound. When she came back, my body was still there, but otherwise I'd left for the day.

Why do I want to put myself through this? I guess it might be the only way to get over it. I find the term 'incest survivor' a strange concept. I cannot believe that this will ever be over. To survive implies an ending. I think we are all marked for life by our experiences. We can get over the initial trauma of dealing with abuse in all its forms, but I believe we are forever shaped by the abuse experience. It will always be an issue. What we can learn are ways of coping with the information rather than forgetting and trying to run our lives on automatic. I can envision a kind of internal wholeness, where I have learned to accept all aspects of myself, even those I hate the most. Although painful, it is also very interesting to go diving for these radioactive nuggets. They are my treasured inheritance.

Joe/Rape Poem

Karen Augustine

Your white hand shoved
up my raw
bleeding cunt
creates gashes
in my endometrium
I a womon gone mad from the repulsion
am bruised
to the deepest blues
at the central point
of my swollen uterus

Rammed through the ache
and the groan and the grunt
Between the scream
in my jugular veins
Above the tear on the
pupil of my eye
Caught in this core of pain
I am witness

straddled on your bed
legs forced apart
arms held down: your
        fucking hand
        fucking violently
inside brown vaginal folds
to
the palest pink

ripped apart
one long evening in November

You remain with me
in the circumference of
my vaginal discharge
in the crimson paste
dried
on the palm of your hand

Your male attempt
to confuse me with images
in fashion magazines

Your male attempt
to use my sexuality
as a device to jerk off

Your male attempt
to measure your self worth
through
humiliation/degradation/violation
within your perverted orgasm
of sexual violence
called rape

MISOGYNIST don't define me by your status/race/class

Here
on this very dark pinch of skin
directly beneath the spit
her warm tongue
defines me as
lesbian

her strong voice
defines me as
survivor
her pulse
thumping against
the weight of our struggle
shoves through
your self-defined systems
your destructive institutions
blood-staining me in a
vocal muscular chord:
stronger than ever

bap/tis/him

Valerie Cain

drop me in
and dip me
    dip me long and hard

make my skin run rivers down my sides
and my tunnel of pain run clean like wet crystal

dip me down
dip me deeper

til we drown that thick tool
still stuck in my mouth
and my throat sings like a bird released

from the jaws of a cat

drop me in   and down   and dip me
so I don't go shopping mid touch

and do it

til i stay

Choices

Richard Hofmann

One of the hardest tests in life is to become the person inside. To find the level allowing us to follow a role that exudes the grace and joy of self truth and value. In life, it appears that a small percentage of young gay men are able to come to terms with the delights of living, in as pure a form as we can find during childhood. For some of us this process becomes one of anger as a result of abuse, sexual or otherwise.

I spent years of my life following a path of drugs and alcohol, all in the name of acceptance and self-image. Through the death of my partner to AIDS as well as my own diagnosis, I have discovered that I am not a bad person, but a victim of my own desire to love and be loved. I became a prey for anyone who would provide a form of love at any price. I cannot regain my lost childhood, I can only grieve and go on with my life dealing with the anger and inability to function on a rational level.

I was born and raised in the city of Calgary, Alberta, a child referred to as a 'bastard' as I was born out of wedlock and grew up in a single parent family of the 1950's. My mother remarried when I was eight years old. My stepfather turned out to be an alcoholic and abusive man. At the age of 12 my parents moved us out of a rental home in a lower income neighbourhood to a brand new house in View Gardens.

View Gardens was an attractive subdivision, with wheat fields and open space surrounding us on three sides. To the south were the majestic Rocky mountains. North was the Calgary International airport. The hub of the neighbourhood was View Gardens elementary, situated on an acre of land with the school at the far north and a playground at the south end.

The playground was used year round, with swings and slides for summer use and a skating rink and shack used in the winter. This shack was where I lost my innocence. It was here that I started my education in gay life, sex and sexual abuse.

In the summer of 1967 I started puberty. Thoughts of naked men hit me about the same time and I found myself overwhelmed with a sense of need to see nude men. I had my first lesson in gay sexuality within days of this awakening.

It was a very warm summer evening when I chanced upon Brad, his brother and another friend, loitering around the skate shack in the park. Brad was a senior at our local high school and his brother was in my class at View Gardens elementary. He called me over and started talking to me. Within minutes he made me feel important, to the point where I would do just about anything for him.

Brad suggested we go into the skating shack and play a game of strip poker. With the belief that I was safe and in good hands, I agreed. The card game ended only when I had lost all my hands and my clothes. Brad started viewing me as a piece of meat to be inspected and eaten. He started in with lewd comments and suggestions of what he and the others would do to me and how they would do it. I became scared and tried to get away, Brad grabbed me and threw me on his lap, laughing and grabbing at my dick and my ass, telling me how much fun I was going to have as they tried to use my mouth and ass as a receptacle for sex.

I don't know why he finally let go of me, whether it was my hysterical screaming, the struggling, or both. I grabbed my clothes and dressed as quickly as possible. I felt humiliated and excited. For most of the next day I kept going over in my head the events of the night before. I stayed physically excited and wanting to explore the feelings of desire that had surfaced. Within two days, I had that chance.

Jock, an 18 year old neighbour, was sitting outside the shack. He called me over and we started talking about school and other mundane subjects. When I sat down next to him, he started putting the moves on me. He pressed his left leg against mine, and after a few minutes he reached over and started running his hand up and down my inner thigh. I was ecstatic, I had found another man to play with. Jock suggested we go inside the shack so as not to be seen. We spent what seemed like hours exploring our bodies. After rubbing each others' dicks with our hands, I couldn't control myself any longer and experienced my first ejaculation. Jock's advances were gentle and sensual, unlike Brad's, which were rough and raunchy. I believed I was in love.

After we had retrieved our clothes and got dressed, Jock asked to see me again. I was sure this was what love was and he wanted to see me again. We discussed how we were going to accomplish this task and came up with what, at the time, I thought was an ingenious plan. I would have his brother take over my paper route and we could use their bedroom while his brother was delivering papers. Ironically, I would never see Jock again, yet I lost my only source of income at the time, by giving away my paper route to his brother so we could be together.

I don't remember how I made contact with Brad again, whether he sought me out or I him. I do know that a part of me will hate him forever. The summer of 1967 was coming to a close, fall was showing through with touches of colour on the trees and the crispness in the air. Brad led me into the field behind my parent's home. He said he wanted to apologize for what happened the first night we met and told me all the things I needed to hear; he thought I was cute and he wanted me all to himself, and that he would take care of me.

While we were sitting in the field, Brad produced a plastic baggie with a wad of Kleenex balled up inside. He opened up the bag and poured in a bottle of nail polish remover and handed it over to me. I told him I wasn't interested and proceeded to give the bag back to him. Brad said trust me and I did. I lost track of reality within seconds of inhaling the nail polish remover. Brad stripped me of my clothes and forced me to suck on his dick and swallow his cum. After Brad got his rocks off, he zipped his fly and left me sitting in the field. I managed to find most of my clothes and got dressed as well as I could. I stumbled home and managed to get into the house and down to my bedroom without anyone spotting me.

For the next few weeks the scene kept repeating itself, Brad would arrange to meet me in the field, get me stoned and shove his dick in my throat and fuck my mouth until he came. Part of me wanted to stop and the other part wanted to keep getting stoned, at any cost. On an early evening in October, Brad suggested we try something different; that we should find a garbage bin and get stoned inside it. We found one behind the elementary school and got in. After getting me sufficiently stoned, Brad started ripping at my clothes, telling me to relax, he was going to fuck me. I tried to get away, but my body wouldn't respond, I had sniffed two large bottles of nail polish remover and had lost all use of my motor functions. As he pulled my jeans down, I begged him to leave me alone. He just laughed and shoved his fat dick in my ass. He didn't stop laughing until he shot his load up my butt. When he finally pulled his dick out of my butt, he told me what a good boy I had been and he had plans for me. I felt something warm running down my leg. As I looked down, I saw a mixture of blood and semen seeping down my inner thigh. I felt pain with each movement of my body as I tried to get dressed and go home. By the time I managed to get out of the garbage bin, Brad was gone. From this point on Brad was no longer interested in me as a play toy. I had now reached the level of commodity.

I became his prostitute. Brad would supply my drugs and alcohol, if I would sleep with whoever he told me to. For the next year I was sold to man after man, so many I don't even remember the numbers. I was forced into almost every kind of perversion men could think of from tying me up and fucking me, to golden showers and scat. The longer I stayed with Brad the angrier I got. The angrier I got, the more drugs and alcohol I consumed. By the time I reached the age of fourteen, the chicken queens had either had me or didn't want me as I was getting too old for their tastes. Brad had long since moved on to other conquests and left me alone with my addiction and my need to acquire drugs.

I started renting myself out to anyone who would get me stoned, doing anything they asked just to get high. By the time I hit the age of sixteen, there was nothing left of who I could have been. I was completely burnt out, but that wasn't the end of it.

I was invited to a party in January 1970. Upon my arrival I headed straight for the bar and proceeded to get drunk. Taking me by surprise, three bastards grabbed me and started dragging me towards the bedroom. The more I struggled and screamed to get away the more everybody in the room laughed and egged on the assholes who were dragging me away.

When I woke up the next morning, I had no recollection of the night before. My body was bruised and I found myself lying in a small puddle of blood, semen and alcohol. I got dressed and went home. My parents had gone off to Medicine Hat to visit relatives, I found I had the house to myself. The first thing I did when I got home was head straight for the medicine cabinet. I swallowed almost every pill I could find.

This was my first attempt at suicide, followed in later years by more attempts, until I had finally come to realize that I couldn't do it by myself any more. I joined the members of a 12 step program, and over the years have started to deal with my issues around loss, anger and self-image. I have not been able to forget or remember all that has happened, but I have started getting on with my life, and started to love myself.

Red Running Shoes

Jean Noble

In honour of those who faced hatred on December 6, 1991 and survived...and in memory of those who didn't.

a call for submissions to an anthology 'by and about lesbian and gay survivors of childhood sexual abuse' catches my eye/I and i want to write although i'm not sure what the text will look like by the time i am done. the process of writing is so much like the healing itself — an unknown thing that somehow drives you into it in spite of the unknowns. the entire process of both hinging upon hope and belief in its possibilities. my question...what does it mean to me as a white, working class lesbian to be a survivor of childhood sexual abuse? what are the connections? i know these things are connected for me and i need now to write them. the connections are emotional and sexual and political, both in the means and the ends. health as the subversive goal, hot and heated sex with women as the ultimate in civil disobedience. emotional health too is equally as subversive. to survive sexual abuse, or racism, or classism or homophobia is a subversive act. to interpret that violence is a political victory. to listen and embrace the difference is the beginning of healing. working and playing and fucking and loving and witnessing and trusting are the means to the ends. but even as i sit to write this that old familiar need sweeps over me. i spend 30 minutes cleaning and tidying my apartment, not out of a need to control as i had first thought, but a need to check every nook and cranny and hiding place — to establish my sometimes obsessive territorial claim to safety even though i live alone. to ensure absolute aloneness before i leave the spatio-temporal behind me and climb into my head to experimentally re-write/re-construct/re-live the stories.

only now i know that 'rewrite' is not a complete and honest description of what i am doing because i am in control of my story now. before it was not my story. i had been sent away from it and am only now being allowed to recover it. but i can step in now and change the story and change especially the ending because the ending is different than what i could ever hope it to be. i can be both speaker and audience, participant and witness, author and subject. before I could only be a passive, voiceless victim of the brutality. now i can narrate the story...speak of the survivor...and own the survival. let me begin...

"Once upon a time there was a little girl..."

a strange place to begin. i have always had trouble with beginnings; 'once upon a time' where those far off fairy tale stories begin...they need imagination, hope and belief too. that phrase acts as a cue to give yourself up to what follows. they always end 'happily ever after'. when i was a kid, these stories only bored me. i would try to listen like the others but the magic didn't happen. mostly it was the Father telling the stories and i knew He would have a different story to tell me later. one of shame and embarrassment and guilt and near death (or so I thought) when He ejaculated into my mouth and i choked, passed out, woke later alone and threw up alone over the fence in the back yard. in spite of it i longed for His stories, i would hear it begin and i always hope that the magic would happen. i was always wrong. i grew tall and left home. i can't say 'grew up', i had done that long before. but i did get older and that was the 'magic'. to wait, day in and day out, for the day i could leave. it finally came.

"...very pretty and delicate. she had to go barefoot all summer, because she was poor, and in winter she wore big wooden clogs which made her little ankles red and sore. there was an old cobbler woman who lived in the middle of the village. she sat and sewed a little pair of shoes as best she might, out of scraps and old red cloth. the shoes were clumsy, but still the old woman meant well when she made them for the little girl. the girl's name was Karen. she got the red shoes and wore them for the first time to her mother's funeral. they were not the right kind of mourning shoes, but she had no others, so she put the red shoes on her bare feet and wore them as she followed the poor coffin. then a big, old fashioned carriage suddenly came driving by, with a rich old lady sitting in it who said to the pastor, 'Listen, give me that little girl and i will look after her well'."

i have been a lesbian for as long as i could remember, but i could not remember, until very recently, how that felt. this year i was watching a science fiction movie where one of the heroes is a big strong dyke-amazon woman who fights with as much intensity as her male comrade, and i finally re-experienced the lesbian energy i had always known as a child but could never really own.

...remembering playing at a very young age with an equally young girl from my neighbourhood. i can't recall the details, but i know i got to be the 'boy' because i expressed my 'love' for the 'girl' by cooly flipping an engagement ring to her with my thumb, and lying back on the couch waiting for her to 'get the picture'. children's games really, but i came to experience that rush in my stomach many times since that day. always in connection with women. always sexual. always exciting. always dyke-hot.

...the same rush i felt reading Billy the Kid comic books. him in his white clothes, rescuing (or was it stealing?) women. i spent hours pouring over those comics, not in love with Billy as a boy but in love with the possibilities he provided my already over-stimulated imagination. the heated excitement of playing 'tie up' games in the back yard — me as 'billy', one of the other girls as the 'lady' tied up to a tree stump — someone else as 'sheriff' — me secretly wanting to be tied up as well... eventually all of us at one time or another were tied up to the tree. the rush in my stomach so intense i can hardly stand still. those 'games' still generating the same excitement now.

remembering playing under the covers with most of my girlfriends, again that familiar rush as we touched and explored bodies during sleep overs, wondering now if parents ever knew what was going on. pretending sleep when they came to look. hearts beating. palms sweaty. breath in gasps but not moving until the door closed and we were once again in darkness with only our bodies. a knowing already that this kind of touch was forbidden. but touching in spite of it. there were many forbiddens that everyone else ignored, including grown ups. why should we not touch. it amazes me to think back and remember how sexual we all were. we shared that intensity until they got taller and discovered 'boys'. until then though we played — in the back yard, under the covers, in the makeshift forts, in dark and damp hiding places during night time hide and seek. heated. very intense, yet unnamed or dismissed as 'child's play'. for some, not acknowledged at all. for others of us though they are cherished memories of growing up lesbian, growing up both in defiance of, and in spite of, the lies of the adult fucked world around us. then and now, hard and heated and intense 'play' serves as rite/write-of-passage that nobody's morality has the right to deny.

"...Karen thought she had the red shoes to thank for her good fortune, but the old lady said they were dreadful, and she had them burnt. Then, on day, the Queen came travelling through the country, and her little daughter the princess was with her. People came flocking to stand outside the castle and Karen was among them. The little princess stood on a balcony so that they could see her, dressed in white. She had no train or golden crown, but she was wearing beautiful red shoes...

By now Karen was old enough to be confirmed. She had new clothes, and she was to get new shoes too. The rich shoemaker in town measured her feet for the shoes; he measured them at his house, in his own room, where there were big, glass fronted cupboards full of beautiful shoes and shiny leather boots, It was all very fine, but sad to say, the old lady could not see very well. Among those shoes was a red pair, just like the princess had been wearing. 'They must be made of patent leather!' said the old lady. 'How they shine!' 'Oh, yes, they do shine!' Karen said. The shoes fit her, and they were bought. However, the old lady did not know they were red. If she had known, she would never have let Karen go to her confirmation wearing red shoes, but that was what Karen did. She was thinking of nothing else when the pastor laid his hand on her head and spoke of holy baptism and her covenant with God, and told her that she must act like a grown Christian woman now..."

remembering how she kept me tied to her by telling me i was so special and so different from the other kids and how she was the only one who understood that, understood me and that i needed her for that. she was always so fucking seductive with me — one time shaving all of her pubic hair off and showing me. me looking, not sure for what or why. but i just kept looking until she put her nightgown down. we climbed into the same double bed that night. i often slept with her only this night i dreamt i was sitting in the bathroom and i wet the bed. then my mother disappeared.

i remember talking to her while she was in the hospital, in the psychiatric ward, but i didn't really know what that was. i only knew she was sick again and had to be in the hospital. i was talking to her on the phone and she sounded funny and i knew she was trying to tell me something but i was scared because i couldn't figure out what that was. she was telling me to mind my p's and q's and i said okay. but i didn't know what p's and q's were. I thought she knew that i tried to run away from Him the last time. i felt bad and said i would be good from now on. i didn't talk to other kids or play any more. i just came right Home to Him after school. it still wasn't enough because one day i came Home and she had left for good — she left the hospital and left the city and was just gone and i knew i still hadn't got it right...

...months later we were out at the bowling alley...me and my sleep-over friends, and the owner came and told me i had to go Home right away so i did and when i got Home i realized my mom had come back only she had a man with her. they fought with my dad, whom we ended up with when she had left. she took us from him, changed our names and within four days we had moved away to Hamilton. she told me of how much this new man loved her but didn't want us but they were going to try it and see if it would work and it would help if i called him 'dad'. i refused. we were far away from Home and yet, during that first year at the new school, i still could not use the public washrooms. that was one of the legacies He left to my body. during fear and intense anxiety my body instinctively seemed to stop functioning; especially whenever my pants came down in public space. my body couldn't distinguish between safe and unsafe public space; all physical space was dangerous. neither could i make the long trip home before my bladder gave way of all it had stored for the day. years later, i spent my first day of high school sitting on the grass at the side of the school because i still couldn't use public washrooms and still couldn't make it home no matter how little I drank. they didn't make it either...he left her eventually. he came back once and was on the outside of the door and she was inside and he was pounding and screaming for her to let him in. she looked at me and i said "don't let him in." she didn't. we packed up what we had and returned to Kingston...back to Home. the first day back, all of us kids were outside and we hear a scream. now i know it is called epilepsy. then we knew she just got sick. so we know she's sick again and the ambulance comes to take her back to the hospital. we are Home. i continue to wait.

my memory is marked so strongly by her absences. it is only now that i am learning to write her presence in my life. we no longer speak. the shroud comes off. i feel raw but i feel. i know something has burst open and i write. i also pee in just about every washroom in my immediate world and write lesbian graffiti on the bathroom walls. the story emerges in bits and pieces as do the memories and they are mine. the shattered bits of me come back too. i write every waking and sometimes half sleeping moment i can trying to put the bits together. once in a while the bits just all fall into place and i see my hand writing on the wall and i know I have come through yet another circle. i have returned home in a whole new way. i no longer spend so much time waiting.

"Next Sunday the children who had been confirmed went to their first communion. Everyone inside the church was looking at Karen's red shoes, and all the pictures of the pastors and their wives were looking at them, and when Karen knelt down at the altar and put the golden chalice to her lips, she could think of nothing but the red shoes. it was as if they were floating before her in the chalice, and she forgot to sing the hymn, she forgot to say the Lord's prayer. Then all the people came out of church, and the old lady got into her carriage. Karen was raising her foot to step up after her when an old soldier, standing near them, said 'Why, what pretty dancing shoes!' And Karen could not help dancing a step or two. But once she began, her legs went on dancing and would not stop, as if the shoes had some power over them. She danced around the corner to the church, for still she could not stop. The coachman had to run after her and catch hold of her. He lifted her up into the carriage, but even there her feet went on dancing, so that she kicked the good old lady. When she got home the shoes were put away, but Karen could not help going to look at them now and then.

Now one day the old lady fell ill, and it was said she was near death. She needed care and nursing all the time, and there was no one more closely related to her than Karen. But there was a great ball in the town and Karen had been invited. She looked at the old lady, who was sure to die in any case, she looked at the red shoes, and she thought it would be no sin. So she put the red shoes on and there was no harm in that — but then she went to the ball and began to dance, as she ought not to have done."

...i am remembering the witnesses. i have never been able to forget this one. this is not easy to write. the written word sometimes so deceptive. a saturday afternoon and me and my siblings are watching t.v. i have often spent saturday afternoons downstairs with the Father. He is asleep in the 'easy' chair. my friends are playing outside and i am hoping to join them as long as He stays asleep. but He wakes up, says to me "it's time to get away from these 'girls' and watch the hockey game downstairs." He gets up and leaves. my grandmother and mother smile at how wonderful it is that He and i are bonding so nicely. i decide to resist. sitting on the top stair i refuse to go down the stairs. nobody understands. they tell me not to be silly, to go downstairs. i'm clutching the railing crying. "oh for christ's sake" the mother or grandmother yells, "go!" i give up. it's the weekend and they want me to keep Him quiet, not to create a scene. i don't remember what happened next except that it's later and i come back into my body for a split second. He and i are on the couch and something is not right. He is not finished yet. it is not time for me to come back. i need to leave again, i stare at the window in order to make myself leave. only now i see all of my friends. they are crouching in the window watching what He has been doing. i get Him off me, run to close the curtains but it is too late. i am standing dead in my tracks — halfway between Him and the basement door — the one that leads out into the back yard where the witnesses are. i don't know what direction to go in so my body just goes back to Him. later i go outside to the park where they are playing and i walk up to them and they run away. they are no longer my friends. none of us know what to do with what happened. the separation has been made. i go back Home and find one of my favourite toys, a black sports whistle i found and i take it onto the front porch and i throw it against the brick and i totally destroy it. i jump on it until there is only the black plastic bits left. the little wooden ball inside the whistle remains intact despite my efforts to destroy it. i will never forget the feeling of that little wooden ball under my red running shoes. obstinate. stubborn, refusing to be crushed. i faced those same witnesses day in and day out for two more years in my classrooms. children can be so cruel, especially traumatized ones. there were no more sleep overs. no more games. no more playing. they are as afraid of me as i am of them. i trust absolutely no one now and i rarely speak. i chew my pencils obsessively at school until my teacher calls my mom and they decide to tape up the ends to keep me from eating the pencil leads. i liked how they felt in my teeth as i crushed them. i crawl up into my head and focus each day on biting through the tape on as many pencils as i can and silently wait. only now i can no longer remember what it is i am waiting for.

"...dance she did and dance she must, out into the dark wood. Then she was afraid, and she tried to take the red shoes off, but they stuck fast. She tore off her stockings, but the shoes had grown to her feet, and dance she did and dance she must. When she danced toward the open door of the church, she saw an angel in long white robes... his face was stern and solemn, and he held a broad shining sword in his hand. 'You shall dance!' he said. 'You shall dance in your red shoes until you are pale and cold and nothing but skin and bone. You shall dance from door to door, and wherever proud, vain children live you must knock so that they will hear you and be afraid! You shall dance and dance!'... One morning she danced past a door she knew very well. She heard people singing hymns inside and a coffin with flowers was carried out. Then she knew that the old lady had died... Dance she did and dance she must, through the dark night. She felt as if everyone had abandoned her, and she was cursed by the angel of god. Her shoes carried her over thorns and briars, and she was hurt and bleeding. She danced over the heath to a lonely little house. It was here, she knew that the executioner lived, and she knocked on the window panes and called, 'Come out! Come out! I cannot come in, because I must dance!' 'You can't know who I am!' said the executioner. 'I cut off wicked people's heads, and now I can feel my axe quivering!' 'Don't cut off my head!' said Karen, 'for if you do I cannot repent of my sin!

But cut off my feet, with the red shoes on them.' Then she confessed her grievous sin, and the executioner cut off her feet with the red shoes. As for the shoes, however, they danced away over the fields into the deep wood, with her little feet inside them."

i would like to write here that i have found the lesbian community and that lesbians helped me heal and it was wonderful but i am not ready to write the 'they lived happily ever after' story. i may never be ready to write that. i don't believe that is my story. there is a story that needs to be written though. i have found certain womyn who are as committed as i am to destroying the lies that have served as our lives.

...my most recent relationship ends and i am learning to reach out to womyn in my life for help. i am not doing well and i have little choice but to reach out. and so i reach. my ex-lover decides that she wants to have an affair with a very close friend of mine instead. they are both in vancouver when my friend calls me. she's not interested in having the affair but i don't believe her. she comes to visit me so we can work it out. while she is here, she refuses to see my ex-lover at all. she spends an intense amount of energy working with me. one day she states again that she is committed to my safety and to our friendship and would never do anything to risk it. we have a history of struggle together. we met in a lesbian incest survivor's group and worked out sexual stuff between us. somewhere along the line we made an anti-suicide and pro-survival agreement together. we would see each other through no matter what it took. i look into her eyes and realize she is committed to me and can find sex in other places. she doesn't need to find it in my ex-lover. i don't think i have ever felt anyone totally committed to me and my safety. i pull away from her and she returns to vancouver and tells me she understands the distance. i tell her i love her and that i'm sorry for withdrawing but i need time to process the new story. it is a story i hope to embrace soon. it startles me out of waiting when i think of it and i start to think perhaps i am not as alone as i believe.

and other womyn. we have been friends for years but i don't believe i have ever really trusted her either. i reach to her for support only she lives in the same city as i do and it is complicated. every time i reach out and she supports me i withdraw and treat her like shit for days after... remembering my younger brother and how he used to make friends. he would see a boy that he thought he might want to be friends with and pick a fight with him on the way home from school. if the boy fought back, my brother would keep him as a friend. if the boy didn't fight back, my brother just continued to beat him up and then walked away. one day my friend called me up — yelled and cried and told me to stop treating her so badly. that she wanted to be my friend and understand and be on my side. she said she couldn't continue if i kept emotionally abusing her every time i accepted caring from her. i cried and she cried and i finally believed she cares because she was willing to fight me to prove it. i tell her too that i love her and i slowly came to realize that i don't need to fight in order to trust. i realize a could just take my time and trust without the fight.

and yet another womyn. we spent years drinking together; drinking in the evenings and telling drinking stories during the day. we did not speak of feelings nor of pain or grief. now, years later we speak of lost families, of trust and safety and love and loyalty to each other. neither of us drinks so much any more. we do continue to tell drinking stories though only now it is only for the fun of it. the stories usually end with "it's amazing either one of us is alive today, eh?" this is not the happily ever after story but it is a start for me. my relationships with these womyn have changed dramatically over the last year and i start to believe i truly can change the stories. another circle is complete. it was just last month that i finally bought a new whistle. it hangs next to the 'still sane' t-shirt in my bedroom.

"She went to the parsonage and offered to be a maidservant there, promising to work hard and do everything she could. the children all loved her, but whenever they talked about pretty clothes and finery, and said it must be lovely to look like a queen, Karen shook her head. When Sunday came they all went to church, and she went into her little bedroom alone. Then the sun shone clear and bright, and the angel of God stood before her in white robes. But he was no longer holding the sharp sword in his hand; instead he held a beautiful green branch covered with roses. He touched the ceiling of the room with it, and the ceiling rose higher and higher, and a golden star shone where he had touched it. Then he touched the walls, and they opened out until she saw the organ being played and the old pictures of pastors and their wives. There sat the congregation in the carved pews, singing from their hymn books.The church itself had come to the poor girl in her narrow little room — or else she had gone to the church. She was sitting in a pew with the rest of the pastor's household, and at the end of the hymn they looked up and nodded to her and said, 'You were right to come, Karen!' 'It was the grace of God!' she replied.

And the organ played and the choir of children's voices rang out pure and sweet. Bright sunlight streamed warmly in through the window and fell on the pew where Karen was sitting. Her heart was so full of sunshine, peace and joy that it broke. Her soul flew up to God on the sunbeams, and when she came before God's throne, no one asked her about the red shoes..."

...but sometimes i still feel incredible anger at white bread, middle-class womyn coming away from a gathering of lesbians that could pass for 'Noah's Arc revisited' — two by two they sit they speak they laugh they interact with the entire world... leaving without a sense of having met anyone... all i did was encounter these entities... feeling like an anomaly...and yet i wonder what the answer is to that... knowing my own patterns in lover relationships and my own work around connection and separation, knowing my anger comes from a different type of knowledge though too... knowledge that comes from being fucked at such a young age. from feeling like it was part of who i had to be, of what my purpose was. the knowledge that comes from knowing that the surface reality is one thing, the unspoken, hidden reality an entire other matter. and feeling that frustration on a daily basis; wanting some contact that speaks of that hidden reality, wanting something that will cut back the layers of pretence of niceness and sanity and sanitized sex to expose the reality underneath. something that will bleed that rawness of its torment and anguish. to reveal the beauty and power of its intensity... its passion... its struggle. boredom and disdain engulf me as i try to process the evening.

... and yet i know the opposite side of such disdain is fear. loneliness and shame and embarrassment as i re-experience my childhood friends running away from me in the park. and anger. rage because He could have at least made sure that no one was watching. rage because my very precious world disintegrated before my eyes. it was gone and i could never hope to recover it. the outside world had been my safe haven. it was a world where i could play, be strong, touch and laugh and be free of both Him and my mother who wanted me for their own use. and it was gone. weekends came and i stayed in my room. spring came and i felt suicidal. for years later i would experience a strange mix of joy and despair during spring. joy because the world was green again and despair because it also brought out the neighbourhood kids, and that meant the torment would begin again. i am trying to learn not to rage at them for what they saw, but children can be so cruel. even now we pay lip service to difference without truly being able to embrace it. i don't know if i will ever be able to erase the feeling of 'freak' that was cut into me that day. i still cannot embrace a lesbian community without the fear of their 'knowing'. my pain keeps me from feeling like i can belong and feel safe at the same time. perhaps time will help. for me this is the connection: this is what it means to be a lesbian survivor of childhood sexual abuse. it means somehow believing that i can begin to rebuild, in spite of the fear. it means constantly validating the fact that i don't automatically feel safe with lesbians. but it also means believing that the safety and strength i felt as a young lesbian can be recovered in spite of the nightmare that it took away. it means having hope in spite of myself, in spite of cruelty. and it means not having to always having to hide or be ashamed of the scars on my arm. the scars written by the same hand that writes graffiti on bathroom walls. i will never be separated from myself again. lesbian texts in my own handwriting tell me home is embedded in my body, and that healing must occupy the same sight. my lesbian body is the sign marking the beginning of my journey home.

"...and they all lived happily ever after."*

it is not time for the end of the story yet. the irony that we believe we can write the end. yet there are so many endings, so many new beginnings. each time a lost memory is recovered it is the beginning of something new and the end of something old. i am reading other texts of my survival: Elly Danica and Shirley Turcott and i hear them speak of sending parts of themselves away during the rapes in order to preserve those parts of themselves. parts they would need later to feel whole and healthy again. they write of returning later to complete recovery and leave more whole than they could have hoped for. believing that i have sent parts of myself away too only not knowing where or how to go back for them. i re-read my writing for clues and find the following journal entry...

funny dreams last night about something hiding in the books — trying to figure out how to get this person out of the book — like a wizard or something has taken this person's spirit or essence and infused it into a book i was holding in my hands — there was me and someone else trying to decide how to get them out — so strange — the book was almost alive with the feel of this person there — very strange.

the dreams seeming to unreal for me to realize the message in it. only now i take it with me to therapy and cheryl and i work with it and i realize this is my hiding place. i dream again and remember leaving the room in the basement, only it is me but i have no body and i float up the basement stairs into the living room. when i wake up from that dream i know why i was so frantic when my mother left town for the weekend a few years ago and she left me with a key to feed her cat. i took a taxi to her place as soon as i knew she had left the city and had the driver wait. i was picking something up from her apartment and i was determined to get it and got home as safely and quickly as i could. i remember this book from when i was a kid. the Oxford English Dictionary, made up of 26 parts, put together by her and my dad. it was one of those deals from a grocery store where you buy each part once a month and when you have all the pieces you send them away and a leather bound version of this huge dictionary is returned to you. it is about seven inches thick and it was the heaviest and biggest book i had ever seen when i was a kid. nobody ever used it but i loved to stroll through it. my parents built this dictionary long before any of us were born and it seemed magical to me. this is what i frantically stole from my mother's world that day. this was where i hid. this hiding has never been part of what i consciously know to be true and yet it reoccurs in my dreams and my writing and my body tells me this is true. nobody would have ever looked for me there and it has kept me safe.

...the struggle with language, with the word, with the story becomes new again for me as i realize now i am getting ready to re-claim myself from the words. i refuse to let my story end with the child in the hands of the Father. this too is what it means to be a lesbian survivor — to change language and change the word. to go beyond the Father. our own bodies have kept us safe until we are ready to rewrite them. the text will give itself up to us only when we realize it has been ours all along. there is strength in the knowing. there is hope. and there is the chance to begin again. call me dykewomyn lesbian whore butch witch call me athene medusa for i have come from myself.

*the text reprinted is from Hans Christian Anderson, *The Red Shoes*, Neugebauer Press: London, 1968.

Pages 202–203

Louise Karch

Fuck. I'm a textbook case.
I can close my eyes and fan the pages, stop
to find my feelings exposed in
rows and columns
highlighted, boxed, **bolded**, underlined

I'm angry *"Part II, Anger the Backbone of Healing," pp. 122–32.*
I'm pissed off *"Anger as a Stage" pg. 59.*

Set up a safe space. *pages 203–204.*
Have a stop rule. *same sort of thing.*

I need to practice saying stop
to my therapists, and lover.
If they touch me and I'm uncomfortable, I'll say it,
and they'll move away until I invite them back.

stopstopstopstopstopstopstopstopstopstopstopstopSTOP.

Fuck. I'm a textbook case.
I want to see them dead. *a typical reaction.*
He and his assistant. Watching me. Talking about me.
Fucking with my little body.

I'll tell this story *"Breaking the Silence", pp.92–103.*

I want to cry. *never mind, I can't yet.*

Hallmark doesn't have any "I'm sorry your doctor fucked you,
a little girl, when you were coming out of anaesthetic" cards.

Hallmark doesn't have any "I'm sorry your lover tells you
to stop and move away" cards.

Hallmark doesn't have any "I'm sorry your first lover o.d.ed,
and her parents contested her will over the rings you shared,
the rings she left you" cards.

Hallmark doesn't have any cards that say "I know what you did
and I am going to kill you."
Hallmark doesn't say very much.

The Courage to Heal on the other hand, pisses me off.

**The Courage to Heal: A Guide for Women Survivors of Child Sexual Abuse*. New York: Harper and Row, 1988.

Put on a Happy Face
Louise Karch

I think that there is only
one baby picture of me.

Face Value.
Make Up.
Face Lift.

Surgery.
Renovation. Re-construction.
Neighbourhood Improvement Programme.

I would like to remember what happened in school
between kindergarten and grade four.

Face Up.
Face Down.
Interest Rates Falling.

Eye.
I see.

optometrists, photographers, x-ray technicians, surgeons,
orthodontists, speech therapists, ear, nose and throat
specialists, psychiatrists and colouring books.
It's maxillio facial clinic day at the Crippled Children's
Society — a day off school.

Put on a Happy Face

Nose.
The knows nose.
Runny nose. Snot nosed.
Follow your nose. Don't be nosey.
I smell antiseptic.

Sticks and stones can break my bones but names
Fuck Face.
Fat Lip.

Lip
Lip Service.
K.I.S.S - Keep It Simple Stupid.
Lippy. Mouthy.
Keep your trap shut. Open up.
Loose lips sink ships.
Open up Wide. Say Ahhhhhhhhhhhh. Biteyourtongue.

The mouth. The opening. The home of the voice, the tongue, the kiss, the erotic. My first kiss, tears.

Laugh lines.
Crow's feet. Caw, Cackle. Croak!
Old Woman, ugly woman, evil woman, witch.

My mother.
Elective surgery. A nose job. A face lift.
Performed by my last surgeon.

Body language.
Shaking the foundation.
Getting it all out on the table.
The naked truth.

"How old are you?"
"I'm old enough to know better...they don't need to see my vagina."

Put on a Happy Face

I'm seven maybe eight...
I'm choking. I can't breathe. I CAN'T
GET AIR.
A tube is being stuck down my throat. Aghhh. NO
NOT AGAIN.

My thing comes ley trolled.
brea be strang con

Machine.
My body remembers what my mind cannot.
My body remembers what my mind cannot.
I am, I was, unconscious.

Plastic surgeons.
Barbie Dolls.
Pleased to report they have the technology, they rebuild me.
Pioneer men, construction workers.
Thank Gods.

The doctor performs face lifts, wiping away women's
characters, expressions and lives.
My mother wipes out her past, her pain, her expressions,
me.

Mother, daughter,
Patients,
Saving face.

Facing the Aftermath

Charles

My abuse occurred when I was about three or four. I don't remember the exact timing, but there are some things you just know. I didn't remember this until six months ago, and I'm twenty six now. I was in therapy for over three years before I started remembering. Prior to that I was dealing with the emotional and physical abuse in my family; so I had enough stuff to keep me occupied. Sexuality was also a problem to deal with. I am from a Chinese family, and I don't know if there's even a word for homosexuality in our dialect. It was tough going outside the family for help, in our family you just don't do that.

One of the triggers that helped me remember was a female friend, the same age as me, who has a similar past. She comes from an alcoholic family, but the issues are similar and we seem to trigger things in each other. This is both good and bad — good because it's nice to go through it with someone, but sometimes it brings up things I would prefer not to deal with.

My memories started when she began to deal with her abuse. I almost used to wish that I had been abused, because it would explain so much and give me something concrete to go on. I could never understand why I had all these difficulties with intimacy and sexuality that were beyond those of so-called 'normal' dysfunctional people. When she talked about it, little things would come out of my mouth and I didn't really know why I'd said them. My first response was "I really empathize, but I don't think it ever happened to me." Then I noticed that I didn't say it never happened to me, just that I didn't think so.

It only came up gradually in my therapy. We use a psychodynamic model that involves doing relaxation and dreams. When I was in therapy, my abuser came into my relaxation imagery. My therapist said go with this, but I thought it was silly. I didn't want to put him in my mind, and when I left I felt like throwing up. That was my first clue there was something going on. In my exercises with my therapist, he kept on coming into my mind, I would let him get closer and then feel terrified. I never remembered exactly what happened, but the emotions of being abused became very clear.

My memories began to emerge in therapy and in conversation with my friend, and eventually I could put the whole story together. My family was not a well-to-do family, but my parents wanted to buy a house. They rented out all of the house except the little flat we lived in. My abuser was a tenant in the front of the house.

My experiences with him connected sexual abuse with the only affection I ever got. My family was so wound up in its own problems that the children were not a major concern. No one in my family was available, especially not emotionally. My abuser gave me attention and, even though I was terrified, it was better than nothing. So, although this is a really difficult thing to say, I have to say it this way — my abuse was also my first love. It was also my first abandonment.

I didn't have any words at that age to understand this experience. All I had were these humongous emotions. I could barely even comprehend the idea that I was being abused by the tenant in the front room. I know that it contributed not just to my sexual issues and dysfunctions, but also to the fact that I was a loner when I was a kid. I always felt different, in some way I felt very advanced. I was considered a bright kid and all that, but I also had many emotions that came too early to me. Part of me had already been numbed or killed. It was hard for me to relate to a lot of the other kids, I didn't have that playful spirit that kids should have.

The abuse continued for a maximum of a year and happened on twelve separate occasions. I remember when he moved out, I was shattered. I was terrified when I saw him but he was all I had; even now saying goodbye is a big deal for me.

I think the abuse had a big impact on my life. In fact, I can't think of anything it hasn't touched. I was emotionally numb for years and was a very depressed and suicidal child. I didn't actually try to commit suicide, but it was always an option I considered. Only now am I realizing the deep seated emotions that haven't gone away, like fear, anger, sadness and distrust. They permeate my professional and personal relationships, how I view my sexuality, the careers I choose and what I do socially.

My sexual expression was impacted in a profound way. I still have problems with affection. I feel that any form of touch is dirty. It's interesting to compare it with my friend. She became really promiscuous, but I did just the opposite. I closed off and was never sexual. I would just be friends with everyone. Sex was always really task oriented, something I did to sustain a relationship. I felt comfortable with the emotional part, up to the point of being sexual and then I would just have sex to get it over with. I always felt separate. The first time I ever had sex, as an adult, I felt like throwing up. I didn't take any initiative or control, I just did what the other person wanted. My 'self' was just thrown out the window. The bottom line was that sex is still something I do for other people.

My abuse really complicated my coming out process and still raises a lot of questions for me. When I feel lonely and I'm getting ready to reach out to someone, I emotionally prepare myself for abuse. I never expect something healthy or healing to happen.

Seeking out help has been a big issue for me lately. There wasn't any professional help available for me as a survivor. If I was a perpetrator, though, everyone would want to talk to me. If I was a female survivor, I could find more support than I did. But when I looked around for resources for male survivors, there was nothing, and I think I ended up turning a lot of my anger inwards. Eventually, I did find a therapy group, for $30 a session, and I'm not even sure it stills exists. It was by referral only and ran for ten weeks. I ended up in a group with two straight men who had been abused by women.

I don't want to be alone in this struggle. In just having this secret I've always felt very alone, as if no one ever really knew me. I never really knew me either, I was hiding. I couldn't connect with people because I was never aware of this secret I was carrying.

I'd like to tell other gay men that if you think you've been abused, you have. When abuse occurs it never goes away. Sometimes I wish I had never remembered, but I'm also glad that I have. It's a very scary thing to deal with, because as soon as you open up those memories, you can't close them away again. If you don't deal with your experience of abuse, it will permeate all aspects of your life. It's important because until you look at the abuse, you will never really know who you are or who you can become.

Crooked Man

Sapphire

the night was no light,
black.
he came in
light cracking the night
stuck in the doorway
of dark
deep hard.
my father,
lean in blue & white striped pyjamas,
snatches my pyjama bottoms off
grabs me by my little skinny knees
& drives his dick in.
i scream
i scream
no one hears except my sister
who becomes no one cause she didn't hear,
years later i become no one because it didn't happen
but it's night now & it's happening
a train with razor blades for wheels
is riding through my asshole
iron hands saw at my knees
i'm gonna die
i'm gonna die
blood, semen & shit gush from my cracked ass.
my mother, glad not to be the one,
comes in when it's over to wash me.
she is glad glad
satanic glad.

she brings her hand up from between my legs &
smears shit, semen and blood over my mouth
"Now she'll know what it's like to have a baby," she howls.
drugged night so black
you could paint with it,
no moon no stars no god.
the night stick smashes my spinal cord,
my legs
bleeding bandages of light,
fall off.
let me go
let me go
don't tell me about god & good little girls
i want to live
i want to live
my cells crack open like glass
the bells are tolling for me
my name disintegrates in the night
God's a lie
this can't be true.
mother is house (we have a nice house, California ranch style)
brother is the nail we drive thru your heart
do it
do it to her brother
mouse is in the house.
running thru my vagina
& out my nose
saucer eyed bucktooth child
Betsy Wetsy
brown bones
electrocuted.
Tiny Tears
that never dry
hopscotch
hickory dock
the mouse fell off

Crooked Man

the clock
the farmer takes Jill down the well
& all the king's horses
& all the king's men
can't put Jill together again.
crooked man
crooked man
pumpkin eater
childhood stealer

This poem was first published in *Conditions 17* (1990)
under the title "Mickey Mouse was a Scorpio".

Ten Minute Salvation

Z. Love

Here I am tucked away in the toy box. The strings still burn where they were attached to my wrists and ankles. It's over now and all that's left is the pain and shame. My mind is bad, the way it plays each second with perfection. His hands are big and dirty. He always has tiny cuts on his fingertips and small, sharp fingernails. Tonight he had whiskers that scraped my cheeks, my face will hurt tomorrow. It's dark and safe here in my hole. I want to scream, but my throat is sore and I will wake mommy.

I was asleep and dreaming. He came into my room and shook me awake. I knew what he would do. He wanted me to lay on my tummy so he could check and see if I was tight enough for him. He told me I loved it, and when I whispered "no", he hit me. I choked on my blood. Why does he want to hurt me? It burned where he put his fingers in. I wanted to cry, but if I did, he would hit me some more. I lied to him and he believed me. When he put his thing inside me, I felt stretched and impaled on a knife. He pushed it in more and when he heard me make little sounds, he stopped. I felt empty and abandoned. He flipped me over and made me beg him.

I was so scared. He put his whole hand in. I begged him like he wanted. I know what to say now. I don't want to, I really don't. I could feel blood down there. My thighs will be sticky in the morning. It hurts. It rips me open. He called me a slut, a whore, and I believed him. I was breathing fast. My muscles were tensing and I agreed with whatever he said. I felt like my body betrayed me. I wanted to scream and release the tension that he created. I hate him for doing this to me. I hate him. I repeat this in my head. Maybe it will make him go away. He kept hurting me with his hand, and then he put his thing in me.

I tried to bite him, but he told me I was teasing him and only sluts knew how to do that to a man. I gave up. Maybe I will fight the next time. I did what I was told like an obedient dog. He could have my body, but not me. I will never give him me, and he can't take it. God, it tasted bad. My throat ached. He didn't take it out. He left me full at both ends. He said it was because he liked the way I shook around him.

He finally went away saying that I had been a good girl and he loved me. He said "Sweet dreams, angel." When he closed my bedroom door it sounded like a cage door. Left in the dark I crawled into my corner where my toys are. I feel so small and forgotten. All I can think of is "I will fall asleep." I know I will dream of how he hurts me. In the morning, before I go to school, I'll put on make-up like he taught me, and if the bruises still show I'll tell lies.

For now I'm going to stay in my hidey-hole with my bears and the doll mommy made me. I want to sleep thinking of how he doesn't have to hurt her now. I hold Muffin to my face so no one will hear me crying.

Boxing Days: A Story

Rick Hammond

"A stroke," Patrick said. "It's got all the signs of a stroke, I tell you. Pins and needles in the arm, constant headaches, dizziness."

His bland wife nodded in agreement.

"What are you taking for it?" she asked Hammond's mother.

"Well..." Mum began slowly. She lit another cigarette. "Let's see. I have to take something to thin my blood, and then I have something for my headaches, then I have to take something else for my thyroid. They also gave me something for my ulcer. I also have something for my angina. Um, oh yes, then there's the stuff for my arthritis and of course, my nerve pills — I couldn't do without those — and also these um...I can never pronounce it...for the disks in my neck. Oh, what else? I have pills to thin my blood..."

"You said that already," Patrick's wife said. Hammond heard her name but forgot it.

"Did I? Well let me think for a second," Mum said dreamily.

Hammond left the conversation to fix another drink. He was tired and wanted to go home. There were seven in the McGraths' living room: himself, his parents, Patrick and his wife, and John and Fancy McGrath presiding over all. Hammond wanted to see how his sister was doing, so he went down to the basement where she and others were watching videos on the huge screen that Mr. McGrath's fading eyes needed to see.

Madeleine looked at him in silence. Hammond sat down beside her and asked how the movie was. She yawned, nodded and put her head on his shoulder, drifted off to sleep.

Hammond was interested in neither the movie nor the conversation of his brother and friends. He hadn't been interested for a decade of the twenty eight years we'd been having these Boxing Day parties, alternating between the two families' homes every year. This year, by nine, bellies full of the half-good, whole-hearted cooking Mrs. McGrath always attempted, presents unwrapped, we'd sit around making inane conversation about mutual funds, somebody selling frozen meat and, of course, swapping 'sicky stories' about each other's illnesses. Mum usually held court in this department, although this year, Dad was suffering from an inexplicable swollen head, which caused his eyes to recede into their sockets, and Mr. McGrath was going blind because of diabetes. The only apparently healthy one was Mrs. McGrath whose milk-and-roses good looks still lit up a room. Hammond had enough talks already about hospitals and illnesses to last a lifetime, his own. So he sat in the basement, drink in hand, sister on shoulder, until his father shouted down the stairs it was time to go.

Patrick clenched Hammond's hand goodbye, said something about lunch. His wife said nice to meet you and Hammond said same here.

"Where's Madeleine?" Patrick asked. "I haven't seen her since dinner."

She was outside headed towards the car.

We joined her outside and Mum climbed in the back seat, because she was nervous when Dad drove on the highway which led to the family home just outside Ottawa. Hammond sat in the front with Dad. His brother Tom, who hated Madeleine, sat beside her as she rested her head on Mum's shoulder.

We drove down the Queensway in silence for a while. Mum broke the peace after staring silently out the window at the snow.

"Well," she chirped, "wasn't that fun?"

****

Even as a child Hammond could remember feeling different from others his age. There weren't a lot of friends at the awful school he and Patrick attended but the kids on the block, including a pretty girl named Simone, were a welcome respite from the on-going torment he received from classmates. They laughed at his size, his hair, the patch he wore over his glasses to strengthen a 'lazy eye', his clothes.

But there was always Patrick to fall back on. Good ol' Patrick who more than once defended him from school bullies, who walked him to school everyday because they were buddies and buddies helped each other out. In return, Hammond shared with Patrick knowledge he had learned in books.

One day we sat outside on the curb, and Hammond showed Patrick how to burn paper with a magnifying glass.

"It's not going to burn," he said.

"Sure it will."

"I don't believe you can make paper burn with glass."

"Just watch."

And it did, does.

Another day Patrick wasn't there, his family had moved to Yellowknife for four years. The impact, of course, was a feeling of abandonment, maybe a feeling that can't be forgiven in some ways.

Hammond was on his own.

****

It is here that memory recedes from the shoreline, returns to the beach, only to tickle reluctant feet. There are images, yes, but often they are only distant whitecaps upon a boiling storm sea. Here, I struggle with the fact memory is not necessarily truth. We remember what we wish. It's no secret each of us remembers HOW things happened differently, and that often makes for unpleasant discussion. We edit out bad parts; remember selectively or invent to compensate for trauma. We do it on purpose, although nobody likes being accused of lying, but whether it is pride or vanity or denial or whatever one chooses to call it, the reasons are there, are one's own.

In journalism school, I had a professor who always stressed there was no such thing as truth; there were only facts. It is the reporter's responsibility, of course, to present those facts in a tight objective manner, let the reader judge for themselves. And that is virtually impossible.

I sit then and judge the facts of my own life and try to sort out the feelings that accompany them. I try, as I write these notes to figure things out in chronological order, but it doesn't work. Each story has its own particular significance attached to it, even if I cannot supply an explanation for the significance. However, I know the feelings attached to them and they run the gambit from hurt, fear, anger, through claustrophobia and anxiety to guilt and humiliation and back again. They are ad hoc feelings.

It's time to deal with that stuff on paper; to attempt to explain the events of yesterday and how they measure the feelings of today.

****

But when did the McGraths move back to Ottawa? It must have been in the early 1970's, because we were all in our teens.

If he had felt abandoned or betrayed somehow, when the McGraths moved North, those feelings melted upon seeing Patrick again. Patrick had changed tremendously, he had started boxing then and his body was beginning to develop into a fine muscular frame.

Hammond thinks now of a question Mrs. McGrath asked him years later and realizes yes, he was jealous of Patrick. Not of his mind, which had a kind of margarine that didn't spread, but certainly of the body which housed it. He thinks of the proud way Patrick carried himself down the street, the fine carriage, muscles tensing and relaxing under tight jeans. There was something terribly appealing about it, yet something to resent as well.

Hammond had always felt torn with physical jealousy and admiration for those in tune with their physical selves. When he was young, Hammond was 'overweight', and his mother's too-tasteful fashion choices made him an easy target for kids who were allowed to wear jeans and leather jackets to school. Later on, the focus shifted to a series of operations for an intestinal defect. Hammond got bounced from doctor to doctor from the age of two until his mid-twenties before the situation was finally pronounced correct, and a comprehensible explanation was offered. Throughout those years, with all the changes in doctors, the changes in approaches, he had never been able to understand fully what was going on, nor the effects it had on his life. It would not occur to him until years later, the impact it had, why he held back, why he lashed out. It would be longer still before he accepted the responsibilities that came with years of denial and set about mending wounds that had scarred him for so long.

But all that was long before he resolved his feelings toward Patrick.

****

Hammond has been stabbed by he who wields the knife which heals; his body ripped by helping hands. "You'll feel some pain," they've said over and over. "There will be some blood, but not to worry."

He has not accepted responsibility for the flesh; he has not even acknowledged it. To him, all this pain is 'natural'. He is no different from other little boys; nor is there any reason why he should be. He has friends, he plays. He reads. And paints. He runs wild with the dog on endless fields under prairie skies and steals vegetables from the garden. But and but.

There is still pain sometimes. "We have to go on the train," Mum says. "You'll have to go in the hospital again, where they'll try to make you feel better."

"Why does it hurt, Mommy?" He buries his face in his mother's neck in their berth.

"I don't know, Lovie," she says, "but the doctor will make it better, you'll see."

But he doesn't, and Hammond doesn't see, will not for years to come. This operation doesn't go right. Nor does the one after that. Or the one which follows it. The camera pans dominos falling slow-mo.

And there is pain. Cold, physical pain; bullets — in — the — werewolf's — heart — pain. But Hammond acknowledges only pain; not from where it comes.

He gets older, asks questions.

NOBODY knows.

He reads abstracts, articles.

Nothing applies to him.

And he's had how much surgery by the time he's eight? The family has by this time moved back to Ottawa, and he is angry at the displacement although he doesn't say so. He wants to go home. But where is home? More important, what is home? A hospital bed, lying flat, like Mother in front of the television, unable to know what she dreams? Pharmaceutical intrusion blotting out physical, emotional duress? From where?

He doesn't know what 'home' means. He doesn't understand doctors. He doesn't know what 'parents' means either. Who are these people who sign papers permitting guillotines to fall? He doesn't understand.

So he is referred to a specialist. A new word. A new attitude. A new procedure, and a new chance.

"Do you understand what your previous doctor did?" he asks.

Let's call him Dr. Smith. Dr. Smith looks like an ingenue dressed head to toe in white. Hammond thinks he looks like the Man from Glad. Only the garbage bag is different. And we are alone in his office.

"All I know is he hurt me lots of times and he's an awful doctor and I hate him."

"Watch your tongue, you little brat. Dr. Mitchell is a very respected member of this profession, and you have no right, NO

RIGHT, to talk about him at all. No right to discuss him at all, understand?"

Hammond nods, frightened.

"Lie down."

He does as he's told; he always does as he's told.

Hammond's pants are on the floor, and Dr. Smith's skilled fingers do their work. Hammond has been touched there before. It's okay; all doctors do this. Hammond has his eyes closed, always does. This time is different though. He breathes slowly, nostrils taking in the sterile smell of — anaesthesia? — from other rooms. His ears hear the sound of wheels on the floor, and footsteps outside, and people talking and somewhere, somewhere else, someone moaning. Hammond feels things too. Feels cold from the sterility, or maybe because his clothes are off. Or maybe because his parents are nowhere to be found. He feels too, Dr. Smith's hands slowly manipulating his member. His touch feels different and Hammond doesn't like it. But he keeps his eyes shut and doesn't resist the touch.

Instead, he concentrates on flying. He always wanted to fly, and fly in dreams, he does. He likes to dream; fly where there's safety in the sky and nothing can touch you. Only the stars, the sun. Kissed by clouds, he travels to Titan, the largest moon of Saturn — he read about it in comic books and the encyclopedia confirmed it — far away from Earth, where no hands can hurt; no knives can cut. He is intangible in dreams.

Hammond hears a heartbeat. Is it his own? Yes. He hears breathing, but it is not his own. Should he look? No. Doctor's still tugging and pulling. But he opens one eye for a second. Dr. Smith's eyes are themselves closed, and he is breathing in the sterility of the room. He has one hand on Hammond; the other on himself. He makes sounds which appear to come from the deepest core of himself, to which he has gone. He sings the rhythms of the caves.

Finally he asks the doctor, is it over? Dr. Smith says yes, but he has to talk to your parents; you need more surgery.

****

She was born when Mum was 41. Madeleine was a difficult birth, and a substantial increase in Mum's monthly drug bills. Hammond was the 'surprise', because his parents were told they'd never be able to conceive children. Madeleine, however, was the 'miracle'.

Madeleine was, is, certainly the most spoiled of us three. The spoiling came from Father, who picked her up every time she cried and yelled at us every time we fought with her. While he spanked us from time to time, Madeleine never got it because it wasn't kosher to hit girls. (Spankings in our home were a rare and tragic undertaking for Dad anyway, since he had been physically abused by his father).

From here, Hammond remembers mostly sounds. A cacophony of crying and screaming and yelling and teasing. An ongoing operetta in four parts starring Dad—Mum—Brother—Sister. They would start as an insult from brother, a cry of protest from sister, a roar in her defense from Father, swelling and building until Mother, who could no longer take it, would scream for peace. The cries were empty and hollow assertions for control, all crying over one another, sometimes to see who could yell the loudest.

****

She cuts her own hair. She is big and blond and pretty. Her name is Simone. She has, like most kids in the neighbourhood, lived in the same place all her life. They've known each other for eight years, since we were six, and we've been friends a long time. All of them: her and Patrick and Hammond, and all the other kids on the block.

But he stands by the window and watches the two of them now, arms around each other's waist. He is excluded from 'the group'. They are no longer a trio. So he watches as Patrick and Simone move off in happy teenage bliss.

He's walked with them; tried to tag along, but they're off on their own agenda, as they should be. To a dance, bowling, dinner. And just like that, it's over. Nine months. The birth of a relationship suddenly abandoned.

Hammond leaps to the rescue.

What was over in nine months for Patrick and Simone, blossoms into five years for her and Hammond. They drift apart, return, open and close a business. They open and close a relationship.

Because his parents don't approve of her, it begins silly, clandestine. They tip-toe out of houses, dogs on leashes. They meet in the field behind the school, let the dogs run free. She is the first for Hammond, he for her. Weeks and months go by, and gradually, they grow more assured in each other's bodies. As confidence is donned, clothes are shed and they explore each other's forms.

It's a nice arrangement. They shed clothes, but only their bodies connect. There is touch but no contact. As inhibitions peel away, emotions are still shackled. She is scared. Hammond is too. She says she loves him and he wonders why, but says he, her.

It goes on like this for some time, but they stand together because neurosis is a gesture for them. Her weight, his scars, their armour and the perfect manacles of love.

One day they are sitting at the kitchen table with her family. The kitchen seems a frequent gathering place for French-Canadian families and they spend many fine days there; cooking, eating, arguing, laughing, nursing hangovers and playing trivia games. The house is always full with Simone's family and friends dropping by, there is always laughter and beer overflowing at the table.

Simone's father has a friend called Roman. The two used to work together on the rail road, have remained friends for 25 years, on golf courses and off. He's a funny man, Hammond likes him. He is one of the permanent fixtures at the table.

Simone smiles and cackles with the rest of us, but when he speaks to her, she falls strangely silent, smiles politely. She speaks to him only when he addresses her.

This puzzles Hammond and one day he asks her about this.

She turns her back to him. "When I was a little girl, Roman used to come over and babysit me sometimes. One day I was in the backyard and he put me in the garden shed with him, and closed the doors..."

Hammond strokes her head.

She tells her story, although he doesn't remember everything she said. He doesn't think she remembered too well either.

"Why didn't you tell anyone?" he asks.

"I didn't want to hurt my father."

Hammond tries for understanding her the only way he can admit, "The same thing happened to my sister."

"Oh God, when?"

"Four years ago."

"Do you know who...?"

"You wouldn't believe me if I told you."

****

Fragments of his parents' lives have resumed after Madeleine's birth. Father takes a number of night courses in Public Administration or something. Mother has a job selling jewellery. Hammond attends Scouts meetings, Tom, Cubs. This leaves Madeleine needing a babysitter once a week while everyone is out. The regular sitter isn't available, so one night Mother asks Patrick if he wouldn't mind.

"Of course not, Auntie Estelle," he says.

It's a night just like any other night. We go about our lives, coming home to sleep and resume a day just like any other day.

Hammond undresses for bed when he hears a soft moaning in the next room, and the sound of muffled parents through the wall.

"Is everything all right?" he asks.

"I think your sister's ill," Dad says sternly.

She seems to be in pain. She's squinting in the light, and there's tears, but she seems more frightened than hurt. She only four years old, and doesn't know how to say what she feels. But it obviously scares her to say anything.

"Does it hurt, Lovie?" Mother asks.

Madeleine hesitates through silent tears, nods.

"Let me see dear," Mum says.

But Madeleine squirms, pulls blankets to her neck and shakes her head.

"Let Mummy see, dear," and she pulls the blankets back.

It's as if an anchor pulls a curtain of tension over the room and everyone is drowned in silence, as we stare at the blood on the sheets.

"Did you pee the bed, dear? Did it hurt to pee?"

But Madeleine shakes her head and turns away.

"She's not hurt, I don't think, she's scared," says Father.

"Sweetie, what happened?"

Madeleine says nothing. She just withdraws into a fetal position and keeps wiping her eyes.

Mother turns to Dad and says something like, "You don't suppose...?"

"Madeleine, was Patrick in your room?" Dad asks.

Dad asks Madeleine if Patrick touched her, it's okay to tell, because she won't be in trouble and Madeleine says nothing. Dad says come on dear, tell us, and she says nothing. Mum asks if Patrick touched her, it's okay to tell because she won't be in trouble and Madeleine says nothing. Mum says, please dear, tell us, and she says nothing.

She just nods her head and moans softly.

****

It's a full-moon night in the field behind the school. Hammond has the dog with him as always, but he must keep it quiet.

A figure steps across the field; Hammond is startled. He had not expected M. to be wearing a ski mask, but it makes sense, of course, not to be recognized. He had not expected M. to bring another ski-masked colleague with him either. Hammond wonders if things will get out of hand, wonders if four years after the incident, it's even worth carrying through with this. Too, he wishes now that Simone had never caught him with another girl and vowed not to speak to him again. She's the one person who knew everything, who could pull the lid off this long-boiling pot. He can still call it off, but should he?

Hammond stutters "I don't want him seriously hurt, or anything broken. Repeat, keep the crap to a minimum. I only want him indirectly to know why he's being attacked, but I don't want any names mentioned."

"We'll handle it good enough," snorts M.

Hammond sees the shape of the man and his dog across the field.

M. taps his shoulder and motions for Hammond to move off. Hammond chokes something like, "...as quickly and efficiently..." but M's gaunt back is turned and he is walking in the direction of shadows. M.'s friend has disappeared too. Hammond hears a whistle, probably a signal to or from M.'s buddy. There is nothing Hammond can now do, except go and sit on a ledge near the parking lot — a favourite spot of his and Simone's — out of sight. It is as tar-black as night can be and nobody can see Hammond. The dog, however, is white, and he wonders if it can be seen.

Hammond can see nothing. For what seems a long time, he hears nothing. Then, there's a sickening thump of flesh on flesh, a grunt of pain. Patrick's dog, an intimidating St. Bernard, begins to bark and Hammond's dog answers it. Hammond silences his dog as best he can, and lights another cigarette.

But his throat is dry, his eyes water. He can feel a beating in his chest that threatens to erupt. He knows this is the wrong way. His mind reels from one image to the next: from a little girl with blood in her bed, to a Boxing Day party, to a nurse's descending, silencing needle, to the magnifying glass burning paper, to Simone, to Simone and Patrick arm and arm, to a day when we were six years old and very happy on a beach in Nova Scotia...

****

It's the four of us: Mum, Patrick, Dad and Hammond. It's been a strange vacation too; hectic, and we've covered lots of ground. Patrick and Hammond have both lost a few teeth from fighting over candies and comic books or something in the back seat of the car. Although stronger than his friend, Patrick has a few bruises and Hammond smirks victoriously at them. Physically, he has been bested by Patrick several times — but then, defended too from school bullies several times, but he has taken great pleasure in nocturnal sabotage. During the night, he's waited for Patrick to fall asleep, pushed him out of the top hammock-like bunk. Three nights in a row, Patrick's crashed upon Hammond's father, and three days in a row, he's woken with another bruise and wondered why he's fallen out of bed.

But today, unshackled from car and camper they are free. Hammond decides to go off by himself and look for seashells, the kind you can hear the ocean in. Leaving his little collection, he decides to try and teach himself to swim. The water is cold and salty and he is fascinated by it. All his life then and now, he's felt mysteriously connected to water. And perhaps because it's one of the purest, real pleasures in his life, he has never bothered to pursue or explain the child-happy reasons for this ongoing joy. Perhaps these were the days that gave birth to a life-long rule to never explain or analyze anything that made him happy.

This day, however, he is feeling very brave. And even though it's three years away from the day he really learned to swim — his instructor pushed him off the diving board and said "Sink or swim, kid" — he decides to challenge his limits and see how far his six year old arms can carry him out to sea. He starts walking cautiously at first; a little braver with each passing step. He can see remnants of clams and pretty stones scattered here and about, and follows them further and further out. The colours gradually fade as the water gets deeper, slightly deeper, until he can see them no more. The water has come up to his chin, and he stands on tip-toes, hip-hopping along the bottom, only to look straight ahead without swallowing water.

A wave comes up. Hammond loses his footing because he's lost touch with the floor. He's stepped in a hole, and surrounded by water. His feet DO touch bottom, but his eyes are closed and all he can feel is cold all around. He leaps for sunlight, for air, and gasps. But all he's inhaled is more water and he goes down again. He doesn't know what's happening and thinks he's going to die today. He has nothing to hold on to, and he bobs up again to call for help, but nobody can hear with nostrils and mouth full of salt water. The best he can manage is a cough. Once again, he is pulled under, and searches, frantically, for something to grasp.

Suddenly, Hammond's arm is yanked, and he's pulled up. He is wheezing and gasping for air. The salt has stung his eyes and they burn before finally focusing on the saviour who still grasps his arm.

It's him.

****

Hammond is standing beside Patrick who holds his stomach.

"Are you alright?"

"I'll be fine."

"What happened?"

"I got jumped by some guy. I don't know why."

"Did you know them?"

"No."

"What did they look like?"

"They? There was only one of them, a black guy."

"A black...? Oh. Well, never mind. Did they, he, hurt you..I mean, can you walk?"

"Yeah, I'll be fine in a minute; just had the wind knocked out of me, that's all, really. He hit me twice, but didn't really hurt me, because I tightened my stomach muscles."

"Hmmph. Well, let me help you home."

"No, I'll manage. He sure took off in a hurry. The dog started barking, and I guess the size of it scared him off."

"I'll bet it did."

Hammond has very little memory left of that night. He remembers going home and wanting to take a shower, and feeling dizzy and sick. The phone rang, and it was Mrs. McGrath demanding he and his father come over for 'a little talk'. Apparently, 'someone' had told Patrick that Hammond had conspired to have him beaten up. What did Hammond have to say to this, and he'd better have a good answer.

Hammond went with his father to the McGrath's house and now remembers very little of what was said, the interrogation that took place. There was some heated grilling from his and Patrick's fathers, Hammond's denial of any involvement in the incident. There were some accusations of wild parties, of drugs and Mrs. McGrath, who had worked as a secretary at the school, knew about the 'unsavoury types' Hammond hung out with. Hammond struggled with trying to decide whether or not to tell the truth, sat petty-passive outside, raging inside, and wanted to tell everyone to go fuck themselves. But for some reason — fear? — or not wanting to damage his mother's and Mrs. McGrath's friendship, he said nothing. Patrick didn't either. He sat across the room looking bewildered at Hammond who stared back.

And then Mrs. McGrath asked the question he'll never forget "Are you jealous of Patrick?"

"I have nothing to be jealous about."

Whatever hollow victory emerged from that night still eludes him. The event does not haunt, nor should it. Some part of his soul felt justified for whatever had been accomplished that evening. He guessed it had something to do with balancing the scales on behalf of someone who could not defend herself. At the same time, it did not interfere with the relationship between the parents. Although the kids would take their separate paths, the parents would see each other more than ever. Hammond and Patrick now limit their meeting to once a year — Boxing Days.

****

Hammond's mother said to him, "So, do you still think you're gay?"

He said yes.

She said she didn't believe he was and he asked why.

"Because you don't act it."

He asked what she meant.

"Well, you know...you don't talk that way...you don't dress funny...you know dear, that sort of thing."

"My thequinth are at the drycleanerth," he said, and went back to his book.

"Oh, don't talk that way, Lovie, you'll meet a nice girl someday and you'll see."

"Well, I don't think I turned out **that** badly."

"We were always far too lenient with you," she said dreamily, about to reprise the monologue Hammond knew was coming. She stared at the flickering images of the obligatory television set. Television is a great way of never having to say you're sorry. After a moment, she lit a cigarette and asked into space, "I wonder how Madeleine will turn out? I don't worry about your brother you know, he's too independent and can take care of himself. You're too old, and at twenty eight, too stubborn to listen to anything I have to say. But I still can't help wondering about Madeleine. Do you think she'll be okay?"

"Eventually. But she'll have to acknowledge what's happened to her, and go through hell before she evens herself out. I still think you should have put her in counselling."

There was more silence, and then she said drowsily, "I wonder if I should have told Fancy?"

"You should have."

"I couldn't you know, I was too afraid of losing our friendship."

Hammond put down his book, lit a cigarette. "At your daughter's expense? She scarred for life. I'm sorry, but I don't think that's right. It'll be a long time before she lets a man touch her."

"I know."

"Have you ever discussed it with her?"

"I've tried but you can't get through to her," Mum said barely audible.

Hammond turned to stare at her lying on the couch, and was about to say "Why? Why have you both always turned a blind eye and pretended there's nothing wrong? You and Dad claim to be parents and have done the best you could do, you're always reminding us, but that's bullshit. You're definition of effective parenting was a roof over our heads and eating dinner out of our laps in silence every night in front of the fucking idiot box. Two of your kids are fucked, if not for life, then for a good many years to come. There was no emotional support of any kind, no nurturing. It was always 'do as I say, not as I do'. If I did what you did OR said, I'd never want to have children, because they'd spend the rest of their lives running to the medicine cabinet every time trouble was around the corner. We had, I had, to do it myself, not because I rebelled but because you wouldn't see or listen to anything. For the last few years your favourite line has been 'you blame us for everything' and for a while I did. Then I started to take responsibility for my own life and feelings, and you never could let go. No, that failed parent in you kept stepping in and in a mad attempt at compensation refused to let me, us, grow up. Too young to cross the highway; too old to sleep with men any more because that's 'just a phase'. Well, it's a phase that's lasted for ten bloody years. I've made mistakes. God knows, still do, will make many more, and say many silly things along the way, until I get it right, because that's the only way I know how to learn. I make no apologies for it whatsoever. You have, at least, acknowledged mistakes, but even that's been only half-assed and years after the incidents, and has never involved you taking any responsibility. I love you as a person, and because you're my mother, and will always, ALWAYS be there when needed. But I can also say I despise you as a parent, and will never forgive you for what you haven't done."

But she was fast asleep.

****

Hammond has tried to write here of recovery. He means 'recovery' only in the loosest sense of the word, because, of course, there is no such thing. That in itself is denial. The best one can hope in the magnifying glass of memory is change. Change: the acceptance of one's past shards, the willingness to accept cuts and go forth, in the beginning, on broken glass. Change: the distortion of one's fun house past to a microscope of the present, a kaleidoscope of one's future. He looks now through the mirror, sees a kindred soul who knows not yet how to connect the pieces, or that those pieces are even broken. He sees his sister and wonders if she sees him when she sleeps.

Killer Bees

Valerie Laub

I have heard of killer bees
swarming a rabbit, say.
apparently you can't even see
the victim beneath
the frenzied, raging mass.
they jab their stingers in
again and again and again and again.
escape is impossible.
they invade every orifice,
surge up helpless nostrils,
seethe across terrified eyes.
open your mouth to scream
and they bluster right in,
forcing the jaws apart,
jamming the throat.

I am told they can survive
our winters, are travelling
north even now.

i have heard
bees jab
their
stingers in
my mouth
open i can't
even
see
every orifice jammed
again
and
again and again
and
again.

The Shield

Valerie Laub

I am feeling anxious, belly tight, lungs thin and my heart working too hard. I do not feel at ease in my body. I do not feel at ease in the world. To stop and allow the garden its true colours is to grow taut. As if I can't let in enough. As if my trying will only point out how much I have missed, am missing. Even sunsets I always pray to end — some stirring too deep. It's easier to plod, to be busy, habitual, a routine that circumvents decision. Instead of creative life, look down, watch the feet, see that they touch cement.

At the age of twelve I decided to consciously become a child — seeking out puddles to stomp through, climbing trees. Life imposed from the outside. I started to question if this was how people lived? If this was Life? If I was alive? In the questioning I recognize the answer: a child alive in her life needn't ask. Breath drops in naturally.

In my adolescence I became aware of The Shield — high and wide and far as the sky. Invisible. Impermeable. Indescribable. From within The Shield I could see and hear and even touch, but I was separate. I could not be a part of what I saw and heard and touched. I was a universe away, eager but unreachable. The way one feels after a high flight when the ears have not returned to normal, pressure not yet equalized.

I know now that the way through The Shield is to touch true feeling, touch pain, since that is the feeling The Shield was built against. I fight it. Not so much because of the pain itself, as because I believe that for me to feel pain is wrong, ridiculous. I was always smiling as a child, always. Nothing real ever happened to me; which is to say I am not real. And when you're not real, there's no justification for feeling sad.

Sometimes briefly, The Shield dissolves, leaving a child who was repeatedly raped by family members, by those closest to her. For a moment the garden is brilliant. Then reality overwhelms and The Shield is back. I no longer acknowledge that child. She is not me. I was never a child. I was never. Never me. No me. No.

This isn't just fear, it's also grief. That I feel divided from Life is too distressing to know. I have always perceived myself as being so eager to live. Yet always I imposed Life from the outside, translated through writing, through reading. Because the truth is, the pressure never did equalize. Breathing is an act of will I cannot always accomplish.

I Have No Name

Stevi Urben

there is Me & there is You...me Now & you Then

& we ride tandem, sleep double in this cradle of memory. I try to sever the umbilical, plant a thorn in your wrist, bury you like a limbless twin in the safe sleep of forgetfulness because I know...he is inside you (still) and I cannot forget...his touch or the way the red river of life ran in ribbons from the crushed rose between your legs.

"She asked for it."

Rape.

when I look back I unearth this bloodied root. when I begin to feel again, you ache against my ribs in the accordion of birth, begging for breath to fill your dead body. but when I try to speak for you, my lips are fat with the flesh of venom and I cannot rise to the hand of forgiveness.

I know it is time to tell someone...or maybe I just need to forget.

NO!!

It is this silence we have come to break like stale bread.

Because I know that as long as I am silent — I have no name.

Daddy is going to make you feel good

Stefan

"Oh, excuse me, I didn't realize you were in there. Excuse me." Out of embarrassment I try to close the door quickly but he grabs my arm firmly.

"Wait. Don't go. Come in... I was just thinking of you..."

I try to pull away but his grip tightens. He forces me into the bathroom. He pins me up against the wall — his arm over my throat so tightly that I feel I can't breathe and yet too scared to move for fear of him breaking my neck. He locks the door. He looks at me with disgust, anger — madness. My heart pounds, my body trembles. My mind flashes with horrifying thoughts — I don't want to die. Immediately, I try to reason with him. I knew then and there what he wanted. First, I thought — calm him down. This is not the man who sleeps with my mother, the man who claims to love her, the man who wants to marry her. No, I thought, this is a madman — a man who wouldn't hesitate to hurt me.

I compromise with him. I tell him to loosen his grip and that I'm not scared. He loosens his grip. I begin to stroke his arms, his body, his hair. I tell him how attractive he is. I tell him how manly he is and how manly he feels. I tell him he's the kind of man I would want, I fantasize about and would want to be like. His eyes close. His body relaxes as if he's in ecstasy.

With all the force within me I desperately push him away and try to run, but he was too smart for that. His grip tightens. His personality changes drastically. It's that look in his eyes. I fear for my life. I want to scream but I can't...

"You bastard, you tried fucking me around." His hands grope my body, my genitals, my ass. He rips my shirt and pinches my nipples. I begin to cry because I feel too weak and overpowered and afraid to fight. The whole time he laughs, as I feel my clothes being ripped off my body.

"Daddy is going to make you feel good." He then begins to bite my neck, my body.I felt confused. Here I was twelve years old and I knew that I liked men, but is this how it's supposed to feel? For instance, I felt good — my body tingled and I felt turned on. But this isn't how it's supposed to be. I wasn't supposed to be feeling disgusted, used, abused, helpless and dirty.

He forced me to my knees and thrust his hard cock into my groin while gripping my ass. "Yeah, you feel good," he says. I just wanted him to finish. I just wanted him off me. But he wasn't going to let go until he was satisfied.

Suddenly my head was yanked with such force that I hit my face on his knee. "Suck my dick, you black, faggot bastard... suck it." He forced his dick down my throat. I tried real hard to free myself. I even tried to bite him, but he kept thrusting his cock deeper into my throat causing me to gag. I wanted to die. My tears just ran down my face. The whole time I was thinking "Where is my mother? How come no one can hear? Somebody help me please!" But there was nobody there to help me.

He repeatedly kept slapping my face with his left hand while telling me I deserved it. This went on, from sucking his dick to being slapped. Suddenly, he stopped, stroking his dick with a distorted grin on his face.

"I want to be inside you. I'm going to fuck you — hard." My fear intensified. I tried to crawl to the corner to protect myself, but I was too weak and he was too fast. Before I knew it he had pinned me down on the floor on my stomach. He began stroking my asshole with his fingers. I desperately tried to get away and I bit his fingers.

"You bastard." He shoved his underwear into my mouth and proceeded to kick me. "I'll show you. I'll show you how a man does it. I'll teach you how to do it right." I feel his dick penetrating me — the pain, oh god the pain, please god, let it stop. But he wouldn't. The more my body tried to resist, the more forceful and turned on he got. By this time I was too numb and in shock to feel any more. I didn't care any more. I just wanted him to have his way and be gone.

I didn't realize he was finished until he took his underwear out of my mouth.

"God your ass is fucking tight — a lot tighter than your mother's pussy." I tried to get up but his boot forced me back down. He held his boot on my throat. I couldn't see anything but his face, and he had on that mad, distorted look.

"You know what will happen to you if you mention a word to anybody." He pressed his boot down on my throat. "Do you understand me?"

"Yes," I replied.

I lay there in shock, shaking and trying to figure out what had just happened. I didn't know whether he was showing his affection for me or if he was telling me he didn't like me. I did know that he had raped me, and I felt very alone and confused.

Don't touch me

Whyte Ravyn

I shiver when you get too close. I have armour for my body, to protect me from touches. I don't like being touched, you can read too much. I couldn't let anyone know my shame, my greatest weakness. I actually crave it. Being touched.

But if you actually touched me — zap! — you would know. And then where would I be?

I'll tell you, under your heel, that's where. I've gotten in trouble for this before, and now I learned my lesson. If you ask for anything, you can't complain if someone takes a fee for giving it to you. Wanting a kiss gets you a tongue. Liking the massage sets you up for the rape. Asking for a hug can lead to anything. So I won't tell you I want anything. I cut off my arms so I can't reach out in need. I cut out my tongue so I can't ask for anything. And I put armour around my body so I don't feel soft, in case you think I'm hugging you back. So don't touch me, okay? I don't like it and I'll just stiffen on some armour if you try.

I've been having a few problems lately, my body armour is just too small. It's a couple of inches shorter than me and a few sizes too small. I have to be careful I'm not walking around with my fingers or ribs or ears poking out. Why right here, I've spilled my guts all over the place, and now I'll have to spend some time tucking everything back into place. Still, it gets a little sore with all this flinging about, and the other parts of me poking out are sensitive from being exposed to the air. So don't touch me, I'm having a few problems with control right now. Don't touch me.

The Little Things

Whyte Ravyn

It's the little things that bother me, really. The rape itself was not half so bad as having breakfast with my rapist in the morning or, sometime later, thanking him for beating off some schoolboy bully for me.

It's the little things, like when the brother pissed in the toilet and made me wash out my toothbrush after, or when the father was really mad and he dunked my head in the toilet. The brother would come into the bathroom as I showered and peer in the curtain. Then he'd wipe off his ass on my towel and I would have to dry myself with it. Of course I resisted, I wiped off all the excess water — I got the idea from the directions on a Shake 'n' Bake package — and stood over the heating vent to dry myself.

It was burning my feet that bugged me, or worse, that some mornings the father wouldn't turn on the heat at all and I would have to use the damn towel after all. Even before then, I can recall the father calling a family conference to discuss the excess use of toilet paper. I would use lots of it, I couldn't stand to touch the stuff coming out of this body. He limited us to one square if we peed, three if we were shitting. For a while he would supervise us to enforce this.

It pissed me off that he worked in the plant that made the stuff, what did he care if we wasted it? I would stand in the washrooms at school on top of the toilet and watch other girls go to the washroom. Funny, I even did this with a friend who would come into the stalls with me. I wonder if she had a father and brother like mine?

I guess it's not too strange that sometime later I forgot what shit was, and why it was coming out of this body. I kept it under the bed for a while until the mother noticed the smell and took it away. I told her it was the dog's but she didn't buy it. She never mentioned it after, the silence, as always, was deafening.

Little things like that still bug me.

Timesharing

Whyte Ravyn

My body is a timesharing condominium. Don't believe me? — look at my lifeline. See how it runs on my hand, starts and stops, detours to drive you mad — it's hard to tell it's the same line, it's fragmented so early. Maybe you don't believe in reading palms, but this one tells the whole story. I don't even shake hands with people in case they find out.

I didn't know there were other tenants in my body when I took possession but, like the deal on parents, there's no refund or exchange. I wasn't even aware of the problem at first, until strange things started to happen. It's disturbing to wake up/come home/enter freely and of my own will and find the place trashed, the food gone, the beer drained and everything smells of smoke. Not everyone here, it seems, has the same standards of conduct. It wouldn't be so bad if everyone was female, it would be real sweet if we all were lesbian. While the city has posted no smoking areas all over the place, it seems I can't keep one particularly obnoxious addict out of my own body.

Do you know what it's like to be standing in a store, and suddenly you notice your left hand creeping out, taking a piece of jewellery you wouldn't be caught dead wearing and putting it in your pocket? I would be furious, because I knew that when the police came pounding on my door, they would find me, while the resident kleptomaniac would be huddled in the closet giggling to the necklace. It wasn't supposed to be like this, and it didn't start this way.

It started off as a welcome thing; I have to admit I encouraged it. I remember my Dad sitting me down for one of his long talks, during which I sat silent and he punctuated his curses and insults by banging the table. One day, I learned that if I stared at a spot between his eyebrows, he thought I was paying attention. Insert "mmmm" into any pauses I heard, and he thought I was responding. It's a little like learning how to leave your apartment empty, but make it look like someone's home. I could leave this rotten world, my rotten life for a life on the high seas, starring in famous movies, safe in places no one could come to. I frequently ran into nasty men who looked like my Dad and had the satisfaction of chopping them into little bits, or better yet, making them walk the plank.

I would be pulled back to my body — the lights would flicker on the set — and plonk! — back in home sweet home. I never even thought about who was sitting there calling me back when the coast was clear. When I think about it now, I guess it wasn't very fair of me to just go off like that. Then things started to get weird.

They used to be like roaches — when the lights came on they'd all scatter. You'd have to surprise them to get a good look at them. But they got bold. They knew they could get away with more, 'cause I needed them like an addiction. I depended on them to be brave, be social, be angry, be sexual. They were the specialists, and I knew nothing. I could be trying to argue, pursing my lips and trying to keep from shaking, until they come up to me. Sometimes they stood behind, sometimes in front of me, and they'd say cold, colder than Clint Eastwood, colder than my Dad, "Fuck you pig. Don't fuck with me. You don't know who you're talking to" in a voice that did not sound very much like mine and scared the shit out of people. I would be inside thinking "Excuse me? Are you sure this is a good idea?" but they would curse and swear and bang the table. It worked. Scared the hell out of everyone, scared the hell out of me. I hated them. I thought I could use them, but all those years they watched my Dad and learned a lot. I guess they felt different about life than I did, but even knowing that, I didn't get rid of them. I laughed, I cried, I lived, I couldn't have done it without them. Actually, that's not true, I cried a lot when no one else was around, but it was cause I felt so empty, like a drained glass, voided but knowing I should be full.

I retreated further. Sometimes I'd skip whole episodes of my life, like someone unplugged me and then switched me back on. But I didn't get to go anywhere this time, just the hallway or a closet. My life was full of blank walls, undecorated, not for show. I struggled, I tried to gain control, but it was like a crowded office with a task for everyone but me.

I felt like an empty figurehead.

I tried overseeing things more. Too afraid to come out for long, I'd watch things from the back room. Friends, I know, came to see me — but they never made it through the security checks. I would send out messages, but security would cut it apart. I tried sending, well, parables I'd like to call them, about my life. It passed through, and I was happy, even though I vaguely knew I was making up stories. I had no stories, no real ones of my own to tell except broom closets and blank walls, and I guess that if I'd cared much about reality I wouldn't have ended up here in the back room. They'd tell stories, and I told stories, and in the end we had another full-timer keeping track of the ever-changing and contradictory tales I told to different people. They regrouped and segregated different friends to keep the confusion to a minimum.

I'm not patient, so I was getting frustrated in my own voided, desperate and bored way. Would you watch three days of TV static to catch twenty minutes of a show you didn't like, already in progress? That's what life was like. I would anxiously wait for my twenty minutes, but when the moment came, I just wanted to be left alone. I couldn't evict them, but I wasn't helpless either.

I decided to put my foot down and every couple of months or so, I sneak out when they're asleep and eat them. I don't know what you think makes up a personality, but I think that what you eat is what you are. I take the backbenchers first, sneak up on the little critters and swallow them whole. The bigger, scarier ones take longer to digest, some little vipers give me terrible stomach aches. As I digest them, I end up with a new set of memories.

Now I know why I let them wander about on their own. I have memories and feelings I thought would flatten me and bring the sky down on top. But if I spit any part of them out, even just a toenail or a hair, that little piece will go into a corner and get big again. So I keep it down no matter what. It's changing me, I've eaten over half of them so far. I know they're still there inside me, ready to leave if anything goes wrong. Then again, I can call on their talents if the going gets rough. Yesterday someone told me I seemed like a new person. I could only say "Funny you should put it like that."

The Basement

Sophia Kelly

For about a month I lived in the basement, fixing it up with a mirror on the wall and a tape deck. Holly and I played my one tape, 'Air Supply', hundreds of times. I still know the words. It was like being a grown up and having my own apartment.

And I wasn't afraid of the dark there. Pitch black and not a shiver. Sure I had a lamp by my bed that I turned off once I was safely in. But once it was off, the blackness, utter and complete opaque blackness, was fine. Now I think it was because he couldn't get me and I was relieved to be out of his line of fire. I felt different when I discovered residues of him, not only in my body, but in my mind as well.

I was lying in bed on one of the first few nights in the basement. Wanting to lock the door. Thinking the cat needed to be able to come in to use the litter box. Thinking I should leave the door ajar for her. As I was thinking this, he opened the door. He repeated my thoughts back to me, almost word for word, and said he had come down to open the door so I wouldn't have to get up to do it.

Later I locked the door. It was the only room in the house that had a door that couldn't be opened from the other side. Nobody had the key, it was lost. You could get in the room by climbing through the storage space into the equipment room, but only my brother and I knew how to do that, and the cat. 'He' was too big to crawl through. So if I locked the door there, I was safe. I didn't let myself think about what from, but I felt safer there than I have ever felt in my life.

Even now I feel like he is outside my door, ghoulish and huge, with a dead face and evil passionate eyes that say "You know I'll always win." He had a grin that was red and thick lipped. When I draw him I even draw his teeth in red. His mouth was sloppy, clumsily, drunkenly destructive like him. He was killing a bug with a sledgehammer, not seeing where he struck but staring straight at it. So tonight, lying here, I can feel him standing there and I feel I risk my very soul writing this because as I clarify what he looks like, he walks through the door. The horror of the memory of him enters my door. If I let it, the ghost memory will come in, loom towards my bed and lurch in front of my face, staring with a look that clearly sees I know he is gonna get me. A look that bellows into my face, reeking with beer fumes, that "You are powerless and I will hurt you because I want to, because you don't matter, because I need to and you are sexy and evil and mine to do with as I want. I own you and your terror makes me do this."

Psychically I fight him off; my back to the ghoul, my shoulders clenched up around my neck so he cannot touch me unprepared and oblivious. I am never oblivious. I am always acutely aware of his presence, especially at night, in my bedroom, wherever that is. Believing that the minute I relax and go to sleep, he will slip in and strike. Believing in psychic warfare, believing that he owns me, that he has planted something in me that draws him to me wherever I am, whenever I am in bed alone. Even a cat can keep him away. If I had known this fact sooner I would not have stayed with my abusive ex-lover so long. Cats do not demand sex for their presence, they ask only that you hold still so they can sleep. My cat knows how to open my bedroom door. I usually prop it open as the sound terrifies me. Only this man or my cat would come in without knocking this late at night, and I do not know at first which it is.

Stand Up and Be Discounted

David John

When my mother was seventeen, she fled her physically abusive father and joined the air force. At eighteen, my parents married after knowing each other for less than a month. At nineteen, a boy (me) was born, the first of four children in just under two years. My mother promised herself that none of her children would ever know the abuse she grew up with. This is what happened.

Before I was five years old we had moved a total of six times. My mother told me that when I was three she had slashed her wrists in my presence. My father took her to the hospital, leaving me and my three younger sisters alone. The earliest memory I have of myself is walking around alone. When I was four I wandered off and got lost several times; once my parents had to call the police because I had been missing for over twelve hours. This behaviour of self-isolation continues to this day.

At five, my parents had gotten a commitment from the military to remain stationed for at least five years between moves. The summer before starting school, two incidents traumatized me. The first I remember clearly. I, my sisters and the neighbour's kids were playing in some sewer pipes beside the ditch outside our house. The side of the ditch collapsed, sending the metal pipes rolling into the ditch on top of me. I was held under six inches of water for nearly four minutes before being rescued. I still have nightmares of drowning. The second incident I only know about second-hand. I had a six inch rip in my rectum. I think that was the first time I was abused.

Even as I started kindergarten my behaviour was noticeably strange — I was already quite disassociated. The first of many psychiatrists diagnosed me as 'hyperactive' and put me on Ritalin. One recess I can remember a girl explain oral sex to me in quite graphic terms. This was the first time I met another survivor. I can't remember whether we did have sex.

At seven, we moved closer to my father's work. I was re-establishing friendships with other children and my sisters. Since my mother and father were both working we needed baby sitters, and so my mother hired two teenage daughters of a friend of my father's. One was a thief; the other was an abuser.

P. told me if I ever told my parents my mother would have to quit her job to look after the crybaby. I had to stay home because I was bad, while my sisters could play with other children. I had to wear clothing that covered my arms and legs to hide the marks of her violence. One time she went too far and I couldn't hide the results. She had given me a bath and poured boiling water over my feet. She told my parents that I was clumsy and had put my feet into hot water before she could add the cold. She masturbated me regularly, all the time telling me that I was disgusting and beating me at any sign of emotion. She had me perform cunnilingus on her while she was having her periods. I was also forced to carry the things she had stolen from my parents to school for her. At nine, my parents fired her for her thefts, I was relieved but silent.

At eleven, we moved again from Ottawa to Trenton. The kids at school made fun of my accent and I lost my ability to socialize. Again, I went to school psychologists and therapists. This time they believed I was mentally retarded. When my I.Q. tests came back with scores of 160 they concluded I was just shy and a bit bored. No further testing was deemed necessary.

At twelve, I developed juvenile arthritis soon after I started allergy desensitization. I would start complaining every afternoon about feeling sick and my joints aching. Since I never had a fever and previous testing said I was an 'underachiever' no attempt was EVER made to determine whether there was a physical complaint. I had several discussions with the principal about 'attitude' and 'laziness'. By the end of the year I knew my pain wasn't real and I should stop feeling it.

In the first year of high school the doctor took me off Ritalin. The stress of being in a more chaotic environment, coming out to myself and drug withdrawal led to a period of extreme acting out. I took razor blades to my arms, face and legs. I became bulimic and anorexic. I masturbated myself bloody. My parents were disturbed about my suicidal tendencies and brought me to the family doctor.

He sent me to a psychiatrist and a psychologist. I was in weekly therapy the rest of high school. The psychiatrist told me he would give me a "very mild relaxer, much more gentle than valium, non-addictive and you can't O.D. on it." This 'mild' relaxer was Mellaril, a drug only used to treat senility and schizophrenia.

My next few years are quite a blur, probably due to the drugs. Recently I looked into my old yearbook and found that I was very active in clubs, being on the executive in Grade 13. In Grade 10 I had decided (with one year's experience) to go to university for music and I made it. All I can remember is my emotional roller coaster — being very competent one moment, depressed the next, then being funny and entertaining and then being incapable of speech. I had started losing time on a daily basis and would forget both things and people.

At eighteen, I entered university, ended therapy and threw my prescription away. I was set to be a grown-up, but things don't always work out the way you plan. Being a good musician in a small town is not being a good musician at university. I came out first as gay then as Jewish was wasn't fully accepted as either. Nowadays I know that maintaining a 65% average without failing is actually good for university, but then I was devastated. I was finally diagnosed as having arthritis and being anorexic. Some of my feelings were finally being validated. Also, a group was just starting for victims of child sexual assault. I went to a meeting but wasn't allowed in — at that time abuse only happened to women.

After March break I entered a severe, near catatonic, dissociative state. I would stay in my room, not eating, for three or four days at a time. When my parents told me they were moving to Germany and I could come too, I was elated. I had just broken off with my first boyfriend (who I had been with since Grade 10). He told me if I didn't become Pentecostalist he would never speak to me again. He hasn't.

Moving to Germany freed large parts of myself. I was young, handsome and unattached, visiting the cities of Europe. It was okay to feel like a stranger, I was. I had overcome my eating disorders and most of my other self-abusive behaviours and I had a good, responsible job. I was a bit lonely but I had dealt with worse. That's why my nervous breakdown came as a surprise.

It had been nearly seven years since my last catatonic episode. That one had lasted two days, this one lasted a whole week. I was in a psych ward for over a month. Once I looked at a doctor's chart of me when I was out of the room, his diagnosis 'hysteria'. Once more I was on Mellaril, once more told nothing was seriously wrong and once more there was no follow up.

Five years ago I returned to Canada upon the death of my father. I joined a synagogue and several 12 Step groups. Neither could accept me completely. In the synagogue, and the Jewish community, incest, addiction and abuse only happens in non-Jewish households. In 12 Step groups, the presumption is that all the people at the meetings are Christian. After trying to explain my sense of alienation at the recital of 'The Lord's Prayer' and being told that "there is nothing offensive about the words, is there?" — I left.

Now, at the age of twenty nine, I don't have to split myself into different parts for the first time in my life. Most incest survivor groups recognize the male survivors. My synagogue accepts me as gay. The 12 Step Caucus of Lesbian and Gay Jewish Organizations is pushing for 12 Step issues to be recognized in Judaism and for Jewish sensitivities to be recognized in 12 Step organizations. Most important, I am now a member of a survivor's group. I am healing. I will be whole.

Sex at Six

Charlene Williams

I was six years old and lived on a farm in rural Britain. My parents encouraged me to wander around the fields and farms in the area. I enjoyed exploring and if I met another person it was generally someone I knew and felt safe with. I was taught not to take rides or gifts from strangers.

One day a man, who I had seen before working in the fields, stopped me and asked me if I liked babies. At the time I had two younger sisters who seemed like a big hassle to me, so I told him I didn't like babies. For a while he tried to convince me that I did like babies, how cute they were etc., but I insisted I didn't like them. I thought it very strange that he was trying so hard to change my mind.

Then he asked me if I knew where they came from. I told him I did and he showed me his penis.

I had seen one before on a boy and touched it also — but this one on the man looked a lot bigger to me. I was a bit scared of it.

He asked me to touch it. I didn't want to. He kept talking to me in a friendly way and finally convinced me to touch it. It felt soft. I pulled my hand away.

He said "That wasn't so bad was it?"

I answered no, but secretly hoped he wouldn't make me touch it again.

Then he went back to the baby thing again with a different slant. He told me if we had intercourse I would not have a baby because I was too young. I did not want his big penis touching me again. I couldn't imagine where inside of me it was supposed to go. I knew that sex was something adults did, but it was very vague and unfamiliar to me. He kept trying to convince me, not to be scared and it wouldn't hurt.

To prove it he walked over to a sheep and fucked it. The sheep didn't move or try to get away. In fact it kept on eating grass the whole time.

I was amazed and curious — but I still didn't want to have intercourse with him. Finally, he offered me money and I agreed.

We lay inside a barn on some hay. When he thrust his penis inside of me it hurt very much. I complained a bit but he didn't stop. So I screamed and he stopped. I was glad.

We got up and he made me promise never to tell anyone. Then he gave me a really small amount of money like five cents. I told him it wasn't very much so he gave me a few more pennies.

I remember thinking I deserved a lot more money for all that pain.

Although I kept my 'secret' for many years, I never thought anyone would believe me anyway. When I was fourteen, my boyfriend asked me how I lost my virginity. I told him and he didn't believe me. At nineteen, I told my second lesbian lover. She laughed and made jokes about "Charlene's Shepherd". I didn't laugh. When I was thirty, I told a lesbian lover who I trusted. She was the first to listen.

Thinking back on the incident I lie slightly to myself and say I had some control of the situation. This justification makes me feel sick, but at least I feel sane. I agreed to have intercourse for money and he stopped when I asked.

But I really would have preferred to explore sexuality at my own leisure with boys and girls of my own age and size. I did not enjoy the abuse. It was very painful.

For most of my life I thought I was okay about the experience because I didn't block it from my memory. Now I realize that it did contribute in some way to the emotional isolation I've experienced; isolation from myself and from others because I've always had this 'secret'.

Also, I am the last person to talk to for support about sexual abuse. All I can say is "too bad it happened. Now get on with your life". Sometimes I feel heartless.

I wish that when I was six there was someone around who I could trust to believe me and listen. I hope that one day we can all quit pretending that child sexual abuse doesn't happen.

Sexual Abuse by Both Genders

Becca

As a child I was sexually, emotionally and physically abused by my mother; as an underdeveloped pubescent teenager, I was sexually abused by a middle-aged, married, childless couple in whose care I was left one summer. All of these traumatic experiences disrupted my life physically, emotionally and mentally.

During World War II, I was born into a very religious family of Christian persuasion and was the third child, unplanned and unwanted. Not long after my birth, my mother had a hysterectomy to prevent further offspring and a few years ago, she told me that she had attempted to abort me. This information, in part, explains some of her behaviour towards me, particularly as I have come to realize that motherhood was a burden to her.

In early infancy, I developed frequent infections and chronic diarrhoea and thus was labelled a 'sickly' child. Most aspects of the maternal abuse I blocked into my subconscious until I went into therapy seven years ago. The memories, some very distorted but real, show that the abuse was a form of punishment, probably for surviving, but also for being sickly and having a poor appetite. I was caught in a vicious circle, especially over supper time, knowing that if I didn't eat I would suffer, but at the same time, my throat constricted with fear preventing me from swallowing. I was excruciatingly thin and likened to a child who had been in a concentration camp. At the age of seven, we moved temporarily, to another house where there was a lock on the bathroom and my bedroom door. I learned to use both, and the sexual abuse stopped but the fear of my mother continued. To this day, when under stress or personal threat, my throat seizes up, I am unable to eat, and I get abdominal pain and diarrhoea. Now I know why.

At the age of fourteen, there was yet another crisis in our home, and I was left with family friends, a married couple, who had a cottage in Northern Ontario. I cared for these people (now deceased) very deeply as they were like loving parents who showed me much warmth and affection and I trusted them. That trust was betrayed just as my childish trust in my mother was betrayed. Warm hugs and kisses on the cheek turned into sexual caressing, forced oral sex and by Frank, threatened and attempted rape. My body reacted temporarily by developing a form of hysterical paralysis and I was sent home for medical treatment. When nothing was found physically, I was sent back and received more abuse for which I was ultimately blamed as the seducer and the instigator. Those memories never really left me and from that time on I developed a phobia about physical contact with anyone other than innocent babies and children who I believed could do me no harm.

The caresses by Jean did arouse me and also frightened me. Although not aware of the term homosexual at that time, I had been taught that Christianity condemned same-gender physical love to be a sin. While I was mortally ashamed at my feelings, I now believe that it was at that time that I unconsciously perceived my innate nature to love women. That concept was pushed underground for several decades as I strived to be the normal heterosexual that was expected of me, but which riddled me with fear.

My father, a social activist, was devoured by his work and if he did have any awareness of what was going on at all, he must have blanked it out of his conscious self because of an inability to cope with the situation. I know that he loved me, and he was a warm and caring man, but he was unable to demonstrate verbally that love. He died after a long illness which I now believe was caused by the stresses in his life, one of which was his marriage to my mother.

Following high school, I went into training for a profession that involved the caring for children. Deep down, I believe that I wanted to nurture and protect them from the evils that I had encountered. I could also trust them. I also tried to force myself into the socially accepted heterosexual role. With great fear and trepidation, I had a brief affair with a man, became pregnant, learned that he was already engaged and, early on, miscarried spontaneously. Something more died inside me and I became married to my profession, burying all feelings of sexuality.

Seven years ago, I took on a position that involved the care of children with cancer and was required to perform procedures that caused them great pain and discomfort. During that time, I began to feel that I was abusing these children even though their treatments were considered life-saving. It was then that I entered into individual therapy.

I was forced to leave that position of work but took on one that had even greater responsibility and a different kind of stress. I became suicidal, took to drinking too much at the end of the shift to dull the pain and, consequently, became more depressed. I broke down and burnt out. My self esteem was at rock bottom as I felt I had failed in the only purpose that I had for living — my work, for without it I was nothing and a nobody. That was four years ago; a life-time ago, it seems.

Thanks to a great therapist and supportive friends, I survived those early months when I felt I was being sucked down into the putrid mud at the bottom of a dank, dark well. Flashbacks of my childhood abuse had started to surface before all this happened and my feelings of powerlessness, guilt, self-blame, inadequacy and shame were all bubbling over. Each day, it took tremendous effort to get out of bed and take care of my most basic needs. Fortunately, I was accepted into a group for survivors of childhood sexual abuse and that, along with individual therapy, enabled me to start to climb towards health and healing. It was during this time, that I was finally able to face the fact that I was a Lesbian and received strengthening support from my counsellors and group members. This group was time limited so I joined another that was run by a Lesbian-feminist therapist. It was during this group that I was encouraged to make a life-sized effigy of my three perpetrators and was given the opportunity to burn it, thus releasing a great deal of my anger and pain. I met other Lesbian women who had been sexually abused by their mothers and read about other women who had shared these same experiences. Within the last few years, I have heard of workshops and groups that have been formed for survivors of same-gender abuse for both men and women. Although statistics to date show that the majority of abuse occurs by men to girls, same-gender sexual abuse is at last being acknowledged and researched.

Another area of healing that I have entered into is that of therapeutic massage. The cells of our bodies remember just as do our minds and I know touch by men and women has caused me much fear in the past. I will never trust the touch of heterosexual men and only feel safe with those that are Gay. For many years, I did not trust the touch of women, but now I have come to know the non-threatening and caring warmth of a hug from a friend or counsellor and also the professional, non-abusive restorative touch of female massage therapists. One day I hope to have a fulfilling, sexual and loving relationship with a woman, but that will be when I am ready to trust my body to another sexually and when I am able to give back that kind of physical love so necessary for such a union. My climb upwards and out of my putrid well towards the sun, blue sky and fresh air continues and I feel that I am three-quarters of the way there. I could not have done that climb without all the caring friends and professional support that I have received. I thank all those who have been and continue to be a part of my healing process. Because of that process and that support, I now believe that I have a rightful place in this universe. Instead of those internal abscesses, there is a small warm glow of self-worth emerging and I know that life is worth living at last.

My Story

Steven Gauvin

When children are five or six they are supposed to be scared of ghosts and spiders and perhaps even 'the dark'. Me, I was scared of men, being killed and being left alone. At the age of five I had a GHOST friend that lived in the same apartment as my family. I would often go down to visit him, as he always had candies or some kind of interesting trinket that he no longer had any use for. I had never really known my father, and at no time during my early childhood had a man taken interest in me. My GHOST friend was the first.

He would hold me in his lap and tell me wonderful stories. He began showing me sexually explicit pictures in pornographic magazines as he held me on his lap. He told me that this is what he does when his girlfriend comes over. I didn't like the pictures — they made me sick to my stomach. But I liked GHOST to hold me. I felt safe.

He would take out his penis and stroke it while I sat on his lap. GHOST would touch me and tell me how good I felt to him. I didn't like the touching but I liked him telling me how good it felt. GHOST would then get up and masturbate in front of me, climaxing and then ejaculating all over me. He would clean me up, give me a toy and send me on my way.

My friends knew of my GHOST friend but they never knew about what went on in his apartment. I felt as if I was the one to blame for what went on. I thought that if I told anyone I would be in trouble and maybe even GHOST would be hurt. I was protecting GHOST, for I'm sure he never meant to hurt me. It seemed unfair that he would be hurt for my own mistake (or so I was made to believe that it was my fault). After six or seven events, we moved away — my family totally unaware of what had happened.

Three years later, when I was eight years old, I was sexually molested by Garth, my mother's half-brother. He would visit us two or three times a year for a few days and we would play fight in the basement. To this day I don't like fighting, as I am a very passive person. He was a very large man and would lie on top of me and move up and down until I thought I would suffocate. I would scream for him to stop but no one was ever around to hear.

He would play with my belly button and slowly move towards my crotch. Then he would start to rub my penis. I couldn't breathe. Garth would take out his penis and make me play with it. I hated it. I screamed louder, only to make things worse. He would yell at me to be quiet. He threatened to kill me if I didn't shut up. Part of me 'spaced out', went somewhere else. I later learned that such dissociation — the separation or split from the wholeness of an experience, a kind of emotional anaesthesia — is quite common under such circumstances.

One night he came into my bedroom when I was asleep. He took all of his clothes off and began masturbating himself while performing oral sex upon me. I don't think he ever penetrated me, but I'm not sure. By dissociating, I could numb my body and take my mind elsewhere and so endure the abuse. This abuse continued for eight years.

When I was fourteen years old another man abused me sexually when I was visiting him and his wife. He took me out to his wine cellar to show me how he made wine and where he stored it. He planted a 'big wet kiss' on my mouth. I numbed my body and sent my mind elsewhere. He pushed me to my knees and made me perform oral sex on him. He ejaculated into my mouth. Afterwards, to make me feel better, he gave me a chocolate bar. It's barbaric that adults seem to think that candies and material gifts will make kids 'keep quiet' about the abuse they have taken. Since that one incident I have never seen nor heard from him.

I left home at seventeen, at which time I set out to discover myself physically, mentally and sexually. After several years of confusion and self-denial I finally came to the conclusion that I was gay. I suffered from many of the long-term effects of childhood sexual abuse. I had both a fascination with and hatred towards men. I became sexually promiscuous, using men for sex and allowing them to use me. Unable to trust them, I was afraid they would hurt me or abandon me, I would always hurt them first.

My mother and I have a very close relationship. However, since my time away from her, as each day passes I wonder more and more if she too was abused as a child by someone in an authoritative position. She has never made any sexual advances towards me or touched me awkwardly, but I sense she still holds the anger and hate inside of her for someone. I wonder if these may be signs of childhood sexual abuse.

Years later, I realized that these men had wronged against me, not I against them. This realization came when I saw the same thing reoccurring between my younger brother and Garth. The wonderful presents, the frequent visits and phone calls home. I had very strong reason to believe that Garth was going to, or was already, doing the same things to my younger brother. The same things he did to me as a child.

An unforseen power within me gave me the courage and strength to stand up for myself and my younger brother. I pressed legal criminal charges against Garth for his sexual wrong doings against me. He got nine months for eight years of sexual abuse against me. Nine lousy months for all that pain, anger, hate, guilt and fear. I believe some of the court decisions were based on the facts of my homosexuality and my age at the time of the events (I was fifteen and a half when the last event I could recall took place).

I'm afraid that when his time has been served, he will come to get me. Garth is a very violent, manipulative and aggressive man. I have done everything in my power (from name changes to phoney telephone listings) to prevent him from coming to 'get me', but somehow I think he will search me out. I fear he will find me. Why? If I am the victim who has done the right thing by taking him to court and standing up for my rights, why am I still living in fear and running for my life?

I am now studying psychology at the University of British Columbia. My interest in becoming a counsellor is rooted in my frustration with not finding help as a youth. When I was growing up I had nowhere to turn for help with my sexual abuse as a victim. Nor did I have anywhere I could turn for help with my sexuality. I see it as my duty to help out the children of tomorrow deal with their abuse early and to come out of the closet more easily than I did.

I am still struggling to survive, but I am a survivor. I look back when I was angry, full of hate and guilt. I was self-loathing and incapable of having any kind of serious relationship. I was a mess and saw no hope for my future. Now I have taken control — my life is mine, not anyone else's. Some set-backs still exist, but I try to deal with them one day at a time. Surviving is an ongoing, lifetime process. Never, never give up or give in, for when you give in you become the victim.

Picnic

Laura Ardiel

It's no picnic being sexually abused.
And it's no fun having abuse anniversaries that come up unannounced and without invitations.

And yet

You invite me to your
Pristine Puritan Picnic
where
no one smokes or drinks but children are abused on the sly.

one, your daughter
-two, your sister
-three, your cousin
-four, your neighbour
-five...

Picnic.

It's no picnic when

my voice of pain and anger falls on deaf ears and tongues prattle on of
this baby, that new wedding, this that, this that but not

'IT'. Not the abuse. Not the incest.

'It's' no picnic.

Picnic

It's no picnic being ignored, being told my
pain does not exist, or being told nothing...

Your silence is no picnic.

It's no picnic being sexually abused.
It's no picnic remembering.
It's no picnic reliving it.
It's no picnic.

And what is in my picnic basket?
The wicker creaks and moans with
the weight of what — you — have — placed in there.
For when I asked for bread
You gave me stones. When I asked
for love
You abused me   and left me alone

A tisket, a tasket.

Sexual abuse is no picnic.

Dead Wolf

Andrew Griffin

No one owned the neighbourhood sandbox. It was located beside the path that cut across the corner of the field on which all our houses bordered. I suppose it was someone's field and, as we grew, it was carved into lots and filled with bungalows. But to the kids of the Murphy, Carragher, Monaghan and Griffin families it was the common ground on which we built our race-cart track, underground fort and sandbox.

I was sitting in the sandbox with Peter Monaghan, playing with my 'Man from U.N.C.L.E.' dinky toy, the one that fired missiles out of the trunk. Peter was ten years old, two years older than me, the same age as my brother, Thomas, who sometimes held me down and tickled me until I cried.

I heard a bike bouncing toward us down the path. By the sound of the rattling, I could tell it was going fast. When I looked up, I could see why.

It was Thomas and he was riding bare bum. Stark naked. In the full light of day.

I couldn't believe it. We had run around without clothes before, but it was always after dark, or inside, when there were no adults around. But there he was for everyone to see, not wearing a thing.

Peter noticed my brother's nakedness at the same time I did. We were both about to burst-out laughing but, as Thomas got closer, we saw that there were tears streaming down his face. He didn't seem to be aware of us at all. He was hunched over, his eyes fixed firmly on home, pedalling for all he was worth.

Peter and I looked at each other. Something was wrong, very wrong, and I could feel a screaming in my stomach. What to do?

"Did you see that?" asked Peter.

I just nodded.

"Should we go ask your mom what happened?"

I knew we had to, but at the same time I wished we could just sit in the sun and the sand, as if we had seen nothing.

Peter was determined. He grabbed me and started hauling me towards my parents' place, which suddenly didn't seem like my home.

When we got there, several other kids were standing in the driveway. I guessed that my brother's ride through the neighbourhood had alerted everyone.

"Go in and see what happened," ordered Peter.

I just looked at him, something told me to stay where I was.

Eventually, my mother came out and called me in. She told the other kids that Thomas was fine and that they should go home.

I went downstairs and Thomas was there. He had stopped crying.

"Watch out for the wolf," he said and started chasing me around the basement. I laughed and played his game, because I knew he needed it, because I was scared not to.

Eventually, by listening to whispers, I discovered that Thomas had been stripped and hurt by another boy, a seventeen year-old boy named Gerald. I learned that he was a very sick boy, a fruit, and the police had taken him somewhere.

"Hey, wanna see a dead wolf? It's lying right over there in the long grass."

That's what Gerald had said to my brother.

I forget how long it was before my brother stopped playing wolf.

We never talk about it.

And five years later, when I am thirteen and know for sure that I am different, 'fruit' will be the only word I will have to describe myself. I will have only one picture of what that word means: a dead wolf.

Dead Wolf

As puberty progresses, the need to be close to other men grows, but 'that' word doesn't seem to fit the feelings that I have; so, I fall silent, hide my desires, like soft breezes on summer nights, and grow afraid that I will always be as lonely as that dead wolf in the long grass of childhood.

May 1991

Breaking the Silence

Rhonda Hackett

Breaking the silence is my common thread of strength in the woven world between pain and life. My peace comes after silence is broken with sounds of resistance. I fight against being silenced. I struggle against being told not to speak about racism. I also speak up about sexism, classism and heterosexism.

Incest is now the next place I have to lend my voice and address its devastating presence in our lives. For me, the intensity of the issue has reached into my soul. Loving, learning and living did not come easily to my lover and me, because a history of incest was part of the picture.

For me it became too much to handle. I believed that incest was the reason for our relationship's dysfunctions, our arguments and our pain. Because incest was part of my lover's memories and struggles, it was easy for me to believe that my lover was the one with the problem. I thought that I was the one who had to be super patient, sensitive or social. The (ill)logic all came crashing down when I could no longer fulfil my superwoman role. I had run out of protection to offer, and was forced to deal with myself, my feelings and my own emotions. I could no longer obscure myself behind a false mask.

I felt impatient waiting for our relationship to change, when I realized my inconsistency. I believed her when she said she was a survivor of incest, yet I treated her as if she was a victim. After all, I thought, she's had to deal with such horrible things, poor baby. I perceived her as fragile, after all she could not even talk about her pain but passed me scribbled notes about it instead. There seemed to be so many things she didn't know how to do. I was also supposed to be her teacher as well as her protector. I would never challenge her, but try to understand — don't worry,

I'll do it for you, it's okay. When people asked about why she wouldn't speak above a whisper, I would make excuses for her, saying that she's shy, she doesn't like crowds, whatever I thought would protect her. Of course, I also didn't like to hear the criticisms of her behaviour, so I was also protecting myself.

I eventually realized that I had no more excuses. I had run out of rescue remedies, and when I thought things were getting better they really weren't. I remember times when there seemed to be a new crisis, a new memory, or another issue coming up every day or every week. That's when I realized that I couldn't just rescue, I needed to deal.

It was time for some fresh air. I felt like I was drowning in my lover's life. I had lost myself and didn't know what I wanted or needed. I realized that I needed to be taken care of too, by myself as well as by my lover. I sat down to look at my life without my lover and saw very little substance there. I had not taken responsibility for my life, wrapping myself around her world instead, and stifling both of us in the process.

I dug deep inside myself and thought about what I needed from my relationships, particularly this one. It surprised me to see that my behaviour had been negative and disempowering. I was focusing on my lover and her life, as a problem to be fixed, without looking at my own life and my own needs.

As my confidence grew, I could talk about my pain, needs and choices as legitimate, and begin to make changes. I had to focus on giving and receiving love in a balanced way. I had to perceive my lover as equal and capable in our relationship, rather than as a constantly needy person. I had to remember that she was a survivor of incest and that I could not erase that experience from her past.

The first thing I noticed as I made these changes was my surge of emotions, especially anger, at her family, my family, her and myself. I tried to focus on myself, my needs, my options and my responsibilities. I had to create boundaries in my relationship — I didn't have any. I had to say what I needed if I was going to initiate changes in the way I related to her. I made boundaries around my needs, space and self, and it challenged her to do the same. Out of this, a tremendous time of growth began for us. I now can see her from a place of respect, understanding and strength, which is to really see her for who she is and not what I want her to be.

I found that I could deal more easily with the constant growth involved in my lover's cleansing. I could not deal when I was afraid, insecure, or uninformed. I needed a place to talk about my pain, my feelings of rejection, my lack of knowledge and my anger if I was to act as a whole person in my relationships. I needed to break my silence and face my fears. I had to find a person who was not judgmental, but was empowering and would help me take care of myself.

I am filled with joy and pride that we have struggled to survive these difficult times. I am even happier that I have broken the silence for myself and others in writing this.

What Dread Hand?

John David Pastway

This is a photograph of me
and my Uncle Robert:

he is holding me on his lap —
you can't see that he is holding me
for the white squared border obscures his hands

but those hands are there

if you hold the picture upright
and peer down the side,
closely,
you may be able to catch a glimpse of those hands

you must look fast, though,
for my Uncle was a magician

you will also see my scrawny little legs,
and matching scratches on my knees,
complementing the colourful red shorts
my Uncle Robert bought for me on that...
proper day —
the end of the sixth year
the beginning of the seventh

(Tyger! Tyger! burning bright
give thee clothing of delight)

What Dread Hand

As we all know,
birthdays are fun,

a statement justified by our two
smiling
over developed faces

in the background,
members of my family can be seen wandering, listlessly,
unaware that the picture was being taken

I still envision my family
coexisting through a hidden camera —
my Uncle Robert is the not so candid camera man

in the back of the background
you can see — if you look really close —
a long pine wood table
with stalwart legs
and a single oak beam
thrust below the middle;
on the white paneled floor, beneath the table,
are two red stains
smeared by the force of hands
magic hands

fortunately, my mother did not notice the spots for if she
had she would have been embarrassed by the speculations of
others who may have believed her messy

now,
occasionally I look at that picture
and remember how I privately tried to remove
the stranded marks from the white paneled floor

but like Macbeth
I could not rid the spots either

just like I can't rid this picture of
the two smiling faces
the obscure hands
the listless family
and the thought of photographs not yet exposed.

Multiple Personality

Regan McClure

This essay deals with where I think dissociation and multiple personality comes from, why such techniques are used by survivors of childhood abuse, and why they take the forms that they do. I believe people have an unconscious mind that can develop into a fairly complex structure. It can be used as a powerful tool for our self preservation. Multiple personality and other dissociative states are ways that some people can make use of naturally occurring abilities to survive a hostile, abusive and overpowering environment. The social and cultural context of the abused child must be taken into account in order to understand the meaning and form of these defenses.

Multiple personality is officially called 'multiple personality disorder' that can be 'diagnosed' when one person seems to have several personalities, who are all quite different from each other and active in the outside world. I prefer the concept of a multiple personality adaptation or survival mechanism rather than disorder, and I refer to people who use this technique as 'multiples'. I call the different personalities within a single body 'alters'.

The ability to dissociate is not pathological, but a natural part of the human psyche which everyone has to some degree or another. Some psychologists like Wolff (1987) believe that as infants we experience distinct and discontinuous states of consciousness. We see our experiences as a series of film clips where each event is unrelated and unconnected with others. As a part of maturing, we learn to develop a coherent sense of ourselves and our environments over time. The development of our integrative consciousness lets us see relationships and consequences between events that helps us deal with the contradictions and complexities of life. According to Wolff, we must learn to integrate our memory and identity across differing states of awareness.

As we develop this 'integrative consciousness', we're still faced with different roles and experiences, but we can make sense of the world by linking them together in meaningful ways. We are constantly challenged to work around many inherent conflicts in our lives and social roles. For example, we define ourselves in many different ways — as parents, as lovers, as workers, as friends and so on. Being aware of the different roles of adult life and negotiating any conflict is an ongoing process that everyone is constantly engaged in. Among displaced, dispossessed and marginalized individuals social roles can come into intense conflict. For example, as a lesbian I'm pressured to cut off and deny my identity and my role as a lover in much of my life. My identity as a lesbian comes into serious conflict with my roles as a worker or daughter. Socially imposed role conflict has resulted in my denial of my lesbian identity to others and even myself. Role conflicts or compartmentalized identities can be found as the result of many different kinds of oppression, including class, race, cultural identity and gender. As adults, abusive experiences prevent us from building an integrated sense of self and challenge our capacity to process and comprehend all the contradictions of our experiences.

Abuse for children is more than a challenge to their identities and roles because they are still in the process of forming their sense of self. It makes more sense to children to believe that they are dreaming when a caregiver abuses them and awake when their abuser is affectionate than try to link these contradictory events in a comprehensible way. There is also the problem that the child's immediate experience of pain is being denied by others. In other words, it's hard for anyone, especially a child, to wrap their minds around the idea that the adult who loves and protects you is the same person who is cruelly abusing you. Children's minds, being more flexible than adult's, can come up with a good answer to this experience. Multiple personalities develop when experiences, memories and roles are not linked together as different aspects of one set of experiences. Forgetting the trauma of abuse isn't enough when the child needs to adapt and respond to the abuse, so another solution is found. The memories must be accessible in order to learn from them, but kept out of awareness in order to function outside of the abusive context. To do this, different personalities are grouped around different sets of experiences that make sense when examined on their own, and the memories and responses to those experiences are severed from the awareness of other personalities.

> "I am a child, a girl. I am eight years old. I answer to Susan, the name given to me at birth. Afternoon comes and there is evil nearby. I can't remember clearly what it is I fear. But I know who and I hear his footsteps coming down the stairs. No where to go. My eyes close, I drift away. Now I'm Ruthie. I'm five. I like to climb on my climber. I like to play on my sandbox. I like to ride my trike really fast. I'm the fastest! The minutes pass, Susan in Ruthie's world. Meanwhile on the basement floor. His words are angry, his voice is threatening. 'Cooperate!' He pushes her legs apart. 'Spread,' he hisses. Someone has to spread her legs for him, someone has to stay in this little body. Her name is Heather. She is scared all the time. She thinks she is a very bad girl. She wants to be a good girl. Heather remembers what happens in the afternoon. When it gets too difficult, Heather too disappears into a hypnotic daydream world and still another fragment of the little girl's mind is left to deal with him. HIM. That's how I got to be this way." ('E.B.', 1990)

As adults, dissociative experiences are part of our everyday lives. We experience forms of dissociation when we 'trance out' in driving, relax in pleasant daydreams, type, have meaningful religious experiences or use hypnosis as a form of therapy. We should think of dissociation as an ability or skill, rather than a mental disorder. Dissociation, in these and other contexts, can provide us with useful, stress-reducing and meaningful experiences. It serves an important function and can be a healthy element of our strategies for coping in the daily world (Heber et. al., 1989).

For a disempowered, isolated and abused child, dissociation is a powerful tool for coping with hostile conditions.

Children often live in socially disempowering conditions. Children's disclosure of abuse is frequently ignored, disbelieved or punished (Goodwin,1982; Kluft, 1984). Margo Rivera illustrates this silencing of abused children in her recounting of one survivor's story.

> "She tried to tell a neighbour who was kind to her what was happening in her home. The neighbour brought her home to her parents and told them the lies their daughter was spreading about them, and she was beaten severely. She told her favourite teacher who asked her if she was sure she wasn't imagining it. The next year she told the school principal who told her to let him know if it happened again. She told him again, and this time he called the police, who charged her for a sexual offense that is no longer on the books and brought her to a maximum security juvenile detention facility to await trial." (Rivera, 1988)

Children as a group do not have the autonomy to escape violent situations or the social power to compel adults to intervene on their behalf. The degree to which adults abuse children is suppressed information in our society, as few adults are willing to believe the extent to which burning, cutting, scalding, beating, mutilation, sleep and food deprivation and other abuses occur with regularity (Coons et. al., 1988; Rivera, 1988). One survivor of ritual abuse relates how she was tortured by night, but interacted as a 'normal' child at school in the day.

> "I hated to be touched and if someone bumped into me in the hall I would jump away. No one took the time to question me or to probe into what was really happening. There were so many obvious signs of abuse; I wish someone had looked further and questioned me earlier. It makes me angry" ('Cheryl', 1990)

In intolerable situations, where escape is difficult and change inconceivable, children can alter themselves to adapt to their environment, through repression and/or denial and/or dissociation and other psychological techniques. One survivor describes his helplessness to alter his situation, so he alters himself instead.

> "Multiple Personalities — mine anyway — are, or more accurately, have been my creative response to exposure to sickening situations. Like any big pile of shit, you can't carry it all at once. But if you make little trips and carry it little bit by little bit, you'll move it. And shit can sit there and stink or it can be placed in such as way as to help things grow." ('Robbie', 1990).

If an abused child has a strong ability to dissociate, this skill can be used in the battle for physical and psychological survival. Dissociation makes noxious and boring tasks automatic (think of how difficult it is to type or drive when you have to consciously think about what you're doing). It can help a child resolve irreconcilable conflicts, and it offers a partial escape from a painful reality. The memory and immediate effect of catastrophic experiences can be psychologically isolated or be used as a channel of cathartic release for 'undesirable' feelings. (Rivera, 1989). It's important to remember that the process of dissociation is not used without good reason, as the costs of creating and maintaining dissociative states are not to be taken lightly. Consequently, most alter personalities in multiples are created for a specific purpose or role (Coons et. al., 1988; Putnam, 1984; Brende, 1984; Bliss, 1984; Stern, 1984). When abuse is severe and prolonged, the usual pattern of developing one consciousness to link up all our experiences is not as adaptive as dissociation. While a dissociative state as extensive as multiple personality isn't as conducive to long-term growth or psychological health, it helps an abused child survive their environment (Wolff, 1987; Putnam, 1988; Ross, 1990, Rivera, 1987, Coons et. al., 1988). If a child is capable of self-hypnosis, this innate capacity can be used to increase their degree of dissociation (Rivera, 1988; Frankel, 1990; Bliss, 1984).

The way I see it, we develop a definition of ourselves only in relation to our environment, and often use cues about how we interact with others to define ourselves. It's a dynamic relationship. As a child begins the process of self-definition, an environment which contains inherent conflicts and contradictions will create conflict and contradictions in the child's identity. The conflicts that exist in our social and cultural environment are mirrored in the conflicts existing in the abused child (Spiegal, 1984; Kluft, 1984). Even in making analogies to describe and convey the experience, the cultural context is very clear:

> "My body is a timesharing condominium...I didn't know there were other tenants in my body when I took possession but, like the deal on parents, there's no refund or exchange" ('Whyte Ravyn', 1990).

Dissociation is a socially acceptable response (relatively speaking) because it mirrors society's desire to dis/associate from the oppressed child's experiences (Rush, 1974). In order to function, society must maintain the secrecy that hides child abuse. Accepting the fact of child abuse would challenge patriarchal and heterosexist structures (Rush, 1974, Rivera, 1988). Secrecy and submission are the heaviest weights of oppression, so the child mirrors these demands with an analogous internal structure. It's hard on the child, but by responding to the rules of our society, it helps the abused child survive.

The alters in multiple personality adaptations are more than an interesting array of stage characters. They reflect social reality and represent cultural archetypes and symbols. This can take the form of an idealized self, such as fantasy figures, religious personalities (Chase, 1987), and the imaginary, perfect friend (Bliss, 1984). The idealizations depend on the social context, for example, a Western boy has an alter named Martin who is a fearless and adventurous spaceman (Bliss, 1984), whereas the alters of two Indian multiples are Westerners which adopt the class-based, socially desirable manners of the West and prefer to speak English than Hindi (Adityanjee et. al, 1989). Racism is also reflected in white, Western multiples who have evil, sexualized, tough and otherwise stereotypical alters who are named as 'Black' and contrasted with 'White' alters who represent innocence, purity, kindness and nobility. This occurs whether the alter's race is unspecified, as in Truddi Chase's White Catherine and Black Catherine, (Chase, 1987) or Eve White and Eve Black from the Three Faces of Eve (Sizemore and Huber, 1988), or whether the race of the alter is specifically described, as in the protector figure, a black man called 'Mean Joe' in Truddi Chase (Chase, 1987).

Sexist stereotypes can be found in cross-gender alters, who can be found in half of all multiples (Kluft, 1984). Although no systematic research has yet been done, several clinicians have found that women commonly have vulnerable, seductive and compliant personalities which are female and their aggressive protector personalities are male. These personalities act out conflicts and power dynamics which mirror the social construction of sex roles (Rivera, 1989). One multiple describes her inability to cope with her anger, and finds that her father and Clint Eastwood are effective personal and social archetypes to release these emotions that are otherwise 'unacceptable' and too frightening to deal with.

> "I could be trying to argue, pursing my lips and trying to keep from shaking, until they come up to me. Sometimes they stood behind, sometimes in front of me, and they'd say cold, colder than Clint Eastwood, colder than

> my Dad, 'Fuck you pig. Don't fuck with me. You don't know who you're talking to' in a voice that did not sound very much like mine and scared the shit out of people. I would be inside thinking 'Excuse me? Are you sure this is a good idea?' but they would curse and swear and bang the table. It worked. Scared the hell out of everyone, scared the hell out of me. I hated them. I thought I could use them, but all those years they watched my Dad and learned a lot" ('Whyte Ravyn', 1990).

Our society labels multiple personality as a psychological dis/order because it challenges the social order, especially our myths that dis/associate us from the realities of childhood, child abuse, the family dysfunction and male domination. Our culture and family system demand that the child keep the abuse a secret. In response to this, the abused child maintains that social order by dissociating and acting out in indirect ways that adults can pretend we don't understand.

> "Because of the voices or creative safety mechanisms that we developed, we are often not believed. For instance, one of my voices blows imaginary bubbles that are impenetrable; no one can get through them. Other voices would take refuge in these bubbles when the abuse was taking place. An element of fantasy was involved in order to escape what was happening and to feel safe; however, I know the difference between creativity used for survival and what actually happened to us" ('Cheryl', 1990).

Survivors avoid the worst punishments by dissociating rather than disclosing, which ultimately serves the social order. It's a comment on our society that the public facade created by adult multiples, which often has no personal history and tightly contained emotions, is acceptable to us. Responses which challenge the social order receive the quickest punishment, and by labelling them 'dis/orders' we isolate the protest as a private, individual insanity.

Abuse is part of our society as well as our families. While conflict is a natural part of living with others and anger is a healthy and necessary emotion, the dominant North American culture is organized around power and oppression. This reduces the chances of resolving conflicts cooperatively or expressing anger in a positive way. Within this context, we often act out abusively along the path of least resistance. This often means down the scale of hierarchical oppression. It can be transformed into sexual, physical, emotional or verbal abuse and directed towards oneself or others, depending on who is the easiest target. There is some speculation than male multiples are under reported because they may act out their aggression on others and end up in prison — as opposed to being self-destructive and placed in the psychiatric system (Ross and Norton, 1989). White and middle-class men may also use legitimized power over others to release their feelings and thus be more able to avoid detection at all. Women survivors have been noted to be more likely to abuse themselves and direct their anger and conflicts inward (Ross and Norton, 1989). However, these case studies are not conclusive, and more research in this area is needed.

Multiple personality can be understood as an adaptation to child abuse, which reflects the culture and is shaped and channelled by social power structures and their need to maintain secrecy and domination of children. In order to understand this adaptation, we need to look at the experiences of child abuse and give voice to those realities. In the words of a multiple herself,

> "We are often forced to hide parts we would like to be free to express. With freedom to express, freedom to live as you choose to live, you gain your freedom to be whole. When you are whole, you can let your voice be heard. Let all your voices be heard." ('E.B.', 1990).

References

Adityanjee, R., Raju, G., and Khandelwal, S.K. (1989). Current status of multiple personality disorder in India. American Journal of Psychiatry, 146 (12), 1607–1610.

Bliss, E.L. (1988). Professional scepticism about multiple personality: Commentary. Journal of Nervous and Mental Disorders, 176 (9), 533–534.

Bliss, E.L. (1984). Spontaneous self-hypnosis in MPD. Psychiatric Clinics of North America, 7 (1), 41–50.

Brende, J. (1984). Psychophysiologic manifestations of dissociation. Psychiatric Clinics of North America, 7 (1), 41–50.

Cancelmo, J.A., Millan, F. and Vasquez, C.I. (1990) Culture and symptomology — the role of personal meaning in diagnosis and treatment: A Case Study. The American Journal of Psychoanalysis, 50 (2), 137–149.

Chase, T. (1987). When Rabbit Howls, New York: E.P. Dutton.

Coons, P.M., Bowman, E.S. and Milsten, V. (1988). Personality Disorder: A clinical investigation of 50 cases. Journal of Nervous and Mental Disease, 176 (9), 519–527.

'Cheryl'. (1990). Ritual Abuse: An Interview. Rites Magazine, 7(6), 8–9.

'E.B'. (1990). Untitled. Rites Magazine, 7 (6), 13.

Frankel, F.H. (1990). Hypnotizability and dissociation. The American Journal of Psychiatry, 147 (7), 823–829.

Goodwin, J. (1987). Mary Reynolds: A post-traumatic re-interpretation of a classic case of Multiple Personality Disorder. Hillside Journal of Clinical Psychiatry, 9 (11), 89–99.

Goodwin, J. (1982). Sexual Abuse: Incest victims and their Families. Boston: Wright/PSG.

Herber, S.A., Fleisher, W.P., Ross, C.A. and Stancork, R.S. (1989). Dissociation in alternative healers and traditional therapists: A Comparative Study. American Journal of Psychotherapy, 43 (4), 89–99.

Janet, P. (1924). The Major Symptoms of Hysteria. New York: Basic Books.

Kluft, R.P., Braun, Bennett, G, and Sachs, R. (1984). Multiple Personality, intrafamilial abuse and family psychiatry. International Journal of Family Psychiatry, 5 (4), 283–301.

McCarthy, J.B. (1990). Abusive families and character formation. The American Journal of Psychoanalysis, 50 (2), 181–186.

Putnam, F. (1988). The switch process in multiple personality disorder. Dissociation, 1, 24–32.
Putnam, F. (1984). Psychophysiologic investigation of multiple personality disorder. Psychiatric Clinics of North America, 7 (1), 41–50.
Rivera, M. (1990). Multiple Personality: An outcome of child abuse. Canadian Women's Studies, 8, 18–23.
Rivera, M. (1989) Am I a boy or a girl? / Multiple personality as a window on gender differences. Resources for Feminist Research, 17 (2), 41–46.
Rivera, M. (1988) Linking the psychological and the social: Feminism, poststructuralism and multiple personality. Dissociation, 2, (1), 24–31.
Rivera, M. (1988). All of them to speak: Feminism, poststructuralism and multiple personality. Unpublished doctoral dissertation. Ontario, Ontario Institute for Studies in Education.
'Robbie'. (1990) Unpublished autobiography.
Rosaldo, M. and Lamphere, L. (1974). Woman, Culture and Society. California: Stanford University Press.
Ross, C. (1990). Twelve cognitive errors about multiple personality disorder. American Journal of Psychotherapy, XLIV, (3), 348–355.
Rush, F. (1977). The Freudian Cover-up. Chrysalis, 1, 31–45.
Sizemore, C.C. and Huber, R.J. (1988). The twenty-two faces of Eve. Individual Psychology Journal, 44 (1), 53–62.
Spiegel, D. (1984). Multiple Personality as a post-traumatic stress disorder. Psychiatric Clinics of North America, 7 (1), 101–110.
Van der Kolk, B.A. and Van der Hart, O. (1989). Pierre Janet and the breakdown of adaptation of psychological trauma. American Journal of Psychiatry, 146 (12).
'Whyte Ravyn', (1990). Timesharing. Rites Magazine, 7 (6), 12. Also published this volume.
Wolff, P.H. (1987). The Development of Behavioral States and the Expression of Emotions in Early Infancy. Chicago: Chicago Press.

Exploring Legal Options

Carol Allen

My article attempts to provide a general overview of the legal options available to survivors who are considering using the criminal or civil legal system against their abuser. I will also try to provide some insight and analysis on the current laws and the possibility of expanding the rights of survivors to pursue a full range of legal options. Keep in mind that pursuing legal action may not be desirable or available to every survivor. A lot depends on the particular circumstances of a case and the individual's emotional and financial resources.

There are three ways for a survivor to pursue legal action: a civil action for damages, a criminal action for incest, sexual assault and/or assault and making a claim under *Compensation for Victims of Crime Act* (1).

A Civil Action for Damages

If survivors want to sue their abusers for money to compensate for physical or psychological harm, they must use civil law (the law of Torts).

In Canada, Tort law has developed primarily through individual cases. Its principles and rules have evolved over centuries and are not defined or written down in a statute such as the *Criminal Code* (2). Tort law serves many functions: it provides compensation to the survivor, deters the conduct and educates the general public (3). To use Tort law specifically against your abuser you first have to prove that harm was intentionally inflicted upon you.

The most commonly used categories (Torts) are battery, assault, false imprisonment and the intentional infliction of mental suffering. Except for false imprisonment, all the above may be used as a basis for survivors to sue their abusers for damages. You can prove intent if you can show that the abuser wanted to inflict the harm that flowed from their assault. As long as the assault was a voluntary act of the abuser, intention can be proven if you can show that the assailant knew that harm was likely or certain to follow from the assault (4). Intention can even be established when the abuser acts by mistake (5).

In the context of child sexual abuse, proving the abuser's intention to inflict battery, assault or mental suffering is not usually difficult. As long as the abuser was not coerced by someone else and you can establish that the assaults took place, the courts should have little difficulty reaching the conclusion that even if the abuser didn't think about the exact physical and psychological consequences of assaulting a young child, they must have known that harm would result from their illegal assault. What abusers count on is not getting caught, and they use fear, threats and guilt to manipulate the survivor into silence.

The Tort of battery is concerned with protecting the right to individual physical security. Someone can be held liable for battery when they intentionally make harmful or offensive contact with another person. The parameters of what type of action or conduct may be construed as battery are wide enough to encompass any unwanted contact short of the insignificant day to day 'innocent' physical contact that occurs in our overcrowded society.

The Tort of assault also protects an individual from threats of future harm. It is based on the idea that everyone should be free from the *fear* of physical harm. In order to sue for damages for assault, a survivor only needs to show that she or he was threatened or otherwise placed in fear of immediate physical harm. The threats and fears need never have been acted upon. When physical harm does take place, a civil battery and a criminal assault has occurred.

Intentional infliction of mental suffering is the final basis for a civil action for damages that will be discussed in this paper. To succeed in this type of case the survivor must prove actual harm.

The courts will require that there be a visible and provable illness resulting from the assault. To prove the existence of an illness means that you will need to provide qualified medical testimony to support your claim.

A survivor can use any or all of these three Torts to begin a civil action for damages. However, there are a number of factors which may influence your decision about whether or how to proceed. A law suit has the potential to cost a great deal of money in lawyer's fees and potentially in court costs. For example, many people are not aware of the costs of a hearing. In addition; if the abuser makes an offer to settle out of court and the survivor rejects it and elects to continue with the trial and if the final award reached at the end of the trial is less than or equal to the amount of the settlement offer, the survivor may have to pay the abuser's lawyers and court costs from the day the offer was made. However, if the judgement at the end of the trial is greater than the amount paid into court, it is likely that the abuser will be asked to pay part of the survivor's costs. Also, legal aid in Ontario is not available for people launching civil actions, only for defending yourself against one.

The task of recovering any money awarded for damages should be carefully considered. In far too many cases, survivors who sue successfully never recover any of the money awarded to them in damages. This can occur if the abuser has no assets or uses technical legal strategies to avoid paying. Getting the money may cost survivors more in legal fees than the money they expect to receive. While the moral victory may be important to some, usually the whole point of civil legal action is getting financial compensation and legal recognition for the damage of the abuse.

The final consideration is the emotional cost of having to relive the nightmare in a public courtroom. The burden of proof you will have to meet is on a balance of probabilities which is lower than the criminal standard of 'beyond a reasonable doubt'. However, in civil cases, the standard used is often that of the 'reasonable man'. I have no doubt you will see the inherent problem with this. Also, remember that like the defense attorneys in a criminal rape trial, the lawyers for the abuser in a civil trial can be just as insensitive and hostile in their cross examination. All of this is not to say that survivors should not sue for damages, but that you should go into this process with a clear understanding of what lies ahead.

Limitation Periods

A survivor's right to sue their abuser for damages is subject to limitation periods, which vary from province to province. These limitation periods are restrictive, and in Canada they range from one to four years (6). However, there is usually an exemption if the claimant is disabled in any way that prevents him or her from pursuing legal action within the specified time limit. The clock monitoring the limitation period will not run until the disability is no longer a factor (7). The theory behind having a limitation period is that no one should be indefinitely subject to the threat of being sued over a particular act. Over time memories fade and gathering evidence gets harder.

However, it can take many years before survivors may start to remember their abuse. In fact, as his or her memory begins to come back, sometimes with the help of intense therapy, she or he is in a better position to express and testify about the abuse.

In all likelihood there will be no official records and the only witnesses will be the survivor and the abuser. Because the abuser is directly responsible for the physical and psychological damage which lead to the suppression of traumatic memories, it is unfair that the abuser can then claim too much time has gone by to allow a court case. Limitation periods, therefore act as an effective tool which is used by abusers to evade civil liability.

In Ontario a survivor has four years to commence legal action after the last incident of abuse (8). The legislation also provides that:

> Where a person is entitled to bring an action mentioned in section 45 or 46 is at the time the cause of action accrues a minor, mental defective, mental incompetent or of

> unsound mind, the period within which the action may be brought shall be reckoned from the date when such person became of full age or of sound mind.(9)

This means that if the survivor was a minor at the time of the abuse, the four year period does not start to run until he or she is eighteen. If he or she has a mental disability, time does not run until she or he is legally of 'sound mind'. Survivors can try to prove that the four year time limit has not run out because they have only recently recovered from a mental disability which had prevented them from starting their action earlier. If they can successfully establish the existence of the disability, they have four years from the date of official recovery in which to sue their attacker.

The court has a fairly narrow definition of 'mental disability'. Ironically, if survivors have managed to keep a job and function on a day to day basis, they are punished for their survival skills and not allowed legal recourse. In doing so, the court fails to recognize that memory lapses are part of surviving the abusive experience, and not a sign of recovery from that trauma. Using the mental disability provision also requires the cooperation of a therapist, who can testify about your mental disability and recovery. This may be nearly impossible in rural communities. It also is not empowering to try and convince people you have recently been of unsound mind after probably spending much of your life convincing yourself and others that you are doing just fine.

The case of *Marciano v. Metzger* (10) exemplifies this problem. In July 1985 a thirty two year old woman, K. M., began an action against her father for incestuous indecent sexual assault "perpetrated upon her in the form of repeated, regular acts of vaginal intercourse over a period of many years when she was in the range of eight to ten years and continuing until she reached the age of sixteen years"(11). K.M. also named her mother in the action, alleging that she had negligently breached her parental duty. K.M. charged that her mother had failed to take steps to protect her daughter when she knew, or should have known, the assaults were taking place. The jury found in favour of K.M and awarded both general and punitive damages. However, the parent's lawyers then argued that the limitations period should bar K.M. from getting any money for damages. Judge Mahoney agreed and dismissed the case.

K.M. reached the age of majority in 1975 and the *Limitation Act* gave her four years from that date to start legal action against her father for incest and six years for the negligence action against her mother. It took K. M. ten years before she was ready to do so. Realizing the problem raised by the *Limitation Act*, K.M. relied on getting additional time by claiming that she was of unsound mind. Her lawyer tried to get the court to accept a definition of unsound mind as "simple incapacity to appreciate the cause of action and the consequences of delay"(12). Judge Mahoney rejected this definition saying that "courts have, over the decades, been most careful to limit the application of the term to cases of genuine mental impairment.... (The proposed definition) goes almost far enough to permit an argument that mere unsophistication could constitute 'unsoundness of mind' for the purpose of the application of limitation periods. This is clearly not and never has been the law"(13). He adds that he believes that "anyone who is capable of retaining and instructing counsel is of sound mind"(14).

In the alternative, K.M.'s lawyer then argued that incest survivors are a special class of claimants to which no time limit should apply, or that special circumstances should be taken into account. Her lawyer proposed that the 'unique dynamics of the incestuous relationship' inflicts silence, guilt and shame on the survivor. It is only years later that the survivor may realize that a terrible wrong has been done to him or her and that there are legal options available. Only when K.M. became aware of the assaults and the availability of legal options should the four year time limit start to run. Therefore in K.M.'s case the limitation period should not begin until the facts on which a court action would be based have been, or ought to have been, discovered by the survivor. This argument had previously only been applied in cases involving contracts and the Tort of negligence. It had never been used in a case involving Intentional Torts. Judge Mahoney refused to allow the test to apply to K.M.'s case concluding that even if he did, he could not find in favour of K.M. because her lack of awareness of the facts surrounding her abuse had not been proven. Since K.M. had been married, raised three children and held down several jobs she therefore was in the opinion of the court, of sound mind (15). Because K.M. had made a number of disclosures to strangers and friends over the years the court determined that she was aware of both the abuse and its impact.

In a more recent civil case (16), the Manitoba Court of Queen's Bench awarded a twenty three year old woman $175,000 for damages arising out of incestuous sexual assault by her father, which began when she was four years old. He was charged with incest under the *Criminal Code*, pleaded guilty and was sentenced to three years incarceration. She then initiated a civil action for damages arising out of the assaults. In determining the amount of damages the court considered her cost of future therapy, lost income (present and future), and aggravated damages (meaning intangibles such as distress, insult, humiliation etc.).

This case was 'successful' for a number of reasons which may be helpful to survivors who wish to take some form of legal action against their attacker. The *Manitoba Limitations Act* was not an issue because the action began within the time limits set out in the Act. The abuser's guilty plea in the criminal action was also significant because the survivor didn't have to prove that the assaults occurred. Therefore, the issue at trial was solely one of damages.

In Ontario, the *Limitations Act* as it is now written prevents many people from having equal access to the legal system. The age of survivors at the time of assault and the particular nature of childhood sexual assault makes it unrealistic to expect that survivors can understand the facts of the assault, decide to seek legal redress and gather the resources needed to do this before the time limit runs out.

There are two possible ways in which changes to the *Limitations Act* can be made. The first is a challenge under the *Canadian Charter of Rights and Freedoms* (17) and the second is through legislative action.

The *Charter* is part of Canada's Constitution and gives us certain rights and freedoms as individuals and as members of particular groups. It protects us from unnecessary government interference in our lives. All government legislation, like *Limitations Acts,* are subject to the *Charter.* If the legislation is found to violate our rights and freedoms which are guaranteed by the *Charter,* it can be ruled unconstitutional and therefore invalid. The *Limitations Act* in Ontario violates a number of *Charter* provisions and can be challenged as unconstitutional (18). The *Marciano* case discussed earlier is being appealed to the Supreme Court of Canada, and there is reason to be hopeful that the court will find that S.45(J) of the Act violates the constitutional rights of child sexual abuse survivors to security of the person and does not provide equal treatment before and under the law and equal benefit and protection of the law.

On the legislative front, the Ontario government has indicated that changes to the Act are under way. *The Report of the Limitations Act Consultation Group* (19) recommends that time limits be uniformly two years after the abuse or the age of majority is reached, but allows for exceptions in certain cases. For example, if a survivor has incomplete recall or understanding of the facts needed to begin the case, the time limit would not start to run until he or she acquired the knowledge or ought to have acquired it. The report also proposed a thirty year ultimate time limit which would bar any claim after thirty years has passed. Most importantly, they recommend that there be no limitation period whatsoever on sexual assault if the abuser had a relationship of authority, trust or dependency with the survivor. The recommendations also ease the restrictions on survivors who have been assaulted by strangers.

Criminal Law

The *Criminal Code* is federal legislation and applies everywhere in Canada. Many survivors try to pursue their case in criminal rather than civil courts. This may be either because there are no legal fees since the Crown handles the case, or because there is no limitation period.

The most relevant sections of the *Criminal Code* state;

> 151. Every person who, for a sexual purpose, touches, directly or indirectly, with a part of the body or with an object, any part of the body of a person under the age of fourteen years is guilty of an indictable offense and is liable to imprisonment for a term not exceeding ten years or is guilty of an offense punishable on summary conviction.
>
> 152. Every person, who for a sexual purpose, invites, counsels or incites a person under the age of fourteen years to touch, directly or indirectly, with a part of the body or with an object, the body of any person, including the body of the person who so invites, counsels or incites and the body of the person under the age of fourteen years, is guilty of an indictable offence and is liable to imprisonment for a term not exceeding ten years or is guilty of an offence punishable on summary conviction.
>
> 153(1) Every person who is in a position of trust or authority towards a young person or is a person with whom the young person is in a relationship of dependency and who
> (a) for a sexual purpose, touches, directly or indirectly, with a part of the body or with an object, any part of the body of a young person
> or
> (b) for a sexual purpose, invites, counsels or incites a young person to touch, directly or indirectly, with a part

> of the body or with an object, the body of any person, including the body of the person who so invites, counsels or incites and the body of a young person,
> is guilty of an indictable offence and is liable to imprisonment for a term not exceeding five years or is guilty of an offence punishable on summary conviction.
> (2) In this section 'young person' means a person fourteen years of age or more but under the age of eighteen years.
>
> 155(1) Everyone commits incest who, knowing that another person is by blood relationship his or her parent, child, brother, sister, grandparent or grandchild, as the case may be, has sexual intercourse with that person.
> (2) Everyone who commits incest is guilty of an indictable offence and liable to imprisonment for a term not exceeding fourteen years.

Consent is not a defense when the survivor is under fourteen years old for offenses involving section 151, 152 and 153, or in cases dealing with sexual/aggravated sexual assault. However, if the abuser is between the ages of twelve and sixteen or is less than two years older than the survivor, consent may be used as a defense. The abuser also can't argue that he or she thought the survivor was over the age of fourteen at the time of the assault if the charge is laid under sections 151 or 152 or the sexual assault sections. In these cases the abuser would have to prove s/he took all reasonable steps to find out the survivor's age.

If by some chance you are not thoroughly confused by now, let me try harder. Corroboration (other witnesses or supporting evidence) use to be required in order for a charge of sexual assault to be laid. Fortunately, in 1987 the code was amended so that supporting evidence is no longer needed, and the judge is not allowed to caution the jury against finding the accused guilty in the absence of supporting evidence.

How a Criminal Complaint is Made

Complaints must be made to the police. If they refuse to lay a charge, it is possible to go before a justice of the peace and do what is called 'laying an information'. Basically, you are swearing that the offence took place. Once a charge has been laid, a Crown Attorney is responsible for taking the case through the court system. Unfortunately, both the police and the Crown are well known for not taking action. Once the charge is laid, the survivor becomes a witness for the Crown. Ridiculous as it may seem, the assault is now considered to be a crime against the state.

It is difficult to determine the percentage of actual charges laid once complaints are made. It is also difficult to find out the conviction rate where charges are laid. When I looked up incestuous sexual assault on a legal database, I found that the vast majority of cases before the courts dealt with the sentencing aspect of the charge. That means that in most of the cases I reviewed, the Crown Attorney or the defense lawyer was appealing the sentence handed down at a previous trial.

Sentencing

For most people, a conviction means little without an appropriate sentence. While the *Criminal Code* says that the maximum sentence for incest is fourteen years, the case law shows that it is rare for the actual sentence to exceed five years. In their written reasons, many judges acknowledge that incest is a heinous crime, yet in the same breath they give the abuser a suspended sentence and probation.

In the case of *R v. Brown* (20), the incest began when the survivor was an infant and continued into her teenage years. Even though she left home her abuser would find her and continue to sexually assault her. The offender pleaded guilty and offered to work in joint counselling with his daughter. His remorsefulness was noted by the judge. He was sentenced to five years and six months. In our criminal system he is eligible for full parole after serving one third of his sentence, and for day parole after an even shorter time.

What is outstanding about this case, other than the ridiculously low sentence, is that Judge Cosgrove outlines the aggravating and mitigating factors that he used to determine the sentence.

Generally, aggravating factors increase a sentence and mitigating factors reduce it. Judge Cosgrove suggests that aggravating factors include the age of the survivor, frequency of the offence and length of time, the extent of the survivor's corruption, the sexual experience of the survivor, the extent and use of violence, previous convictions, pregnancy, existence of perverted acts, offender's attitude toward the survivor, offender's use of power as father, effects of sex acts upon the survivor and the degree to which the survivor enticed the offender. On the other hand, a sentence can be reduced by mitigating factors such as a guilty plea, the affection the offender has for the survivor, if the survivor had previous sexual experience, if the survivor 'seduced' the father and whether it is in the best interest of the family to give the father a short sentence.

In *R. v. E.* (21) the Crown appealed a trial judge's decision to give a suspended sentence with probation and five hundred hours of community service to a man convicted of incest. The victim was fourteen years old and had been subjected to incestuous sexual assault for a period of seven to eight months. The Ontario Court of Appeal held that the trial judge failed to impose a sentence that fit the gravity of the offence and that there were no mitigating factors involved which warranted so light a sentence. They also found that the trial judge was wrong to view the sexual assault as a consensual relationship because there was no violence and that resulting financial hardship to his family was no reason to not put him in jail. At the time of the appeal the offender had performed his community work so his sentence was changed to eighteen months in a reformatory.

In Manitoba, the Crown appealed a trial judges's sentence of eighteen months plus three years probation of a man who pleaded guilty to sexually assaulting his daughter beginning when she was ten (22). Later she became pregnant, he physically assaulted her and she miscarried. The Court of Appeal increased his sentence to three years incarceration. In Newfoundland, a man pleaded guilty to incestuous sexual assault with his twelve year old daughter over a period of ten years (23). He was found to have used coercion and violence in order to get her to submit. If she refused he would threaten to assault another member of the family and often did. Even though she moved away he pursued her. She attempted to commit suicide. A survivor impact study, done by a psychiatrist and admitted into court confirmed that she had suffered irrevocable damage and was suffering from post traumatic stress disorder and depression. He was sentenced to five years imprisonment.

In an number of recent cases, individuals who have been charged with child sexual assault that occurred a long time ago (ten to thirty years) have invoked the *Charter* to argue that their right to a fair trial has been violated because of the length of time between the alleged assault and the charge (24). In *R. v. F.* (25) the Crown appealed a trial judges decision to stay the prosecution of a man charged with indecently assaulting his common law partner's nine and ten year old daughters and had counselled her twelve year old sons to indecently assault their sisters. The trial judge found that because records and witnesses were no longer available and one potential witness was dead, a trial would violate the accused's right to a fair trial. In a rare moment of insight, the Supreme Court of Ontario allowed the appeal and decided that the delay was not enough to justify stopping the court procedures.

These, and other cases, suggest that when there have been many years between the abuse and the charge it is likely that the abuser will invoke the *Charter's* right to a fair trial. As infuriated as I feel when I read such cases where the accused has done this successfully, I have to remember that the problem is not the Constitutional right that guarantees us all the right to a fair and impartial trial within a reasonable time. The problem is in how these Constitutional rights are interpreted by the courts when dealing with cases of child sexual assault.

Criminal Injuries Compensation

In Ontario, the *Compensation for Victims of Crime Act* section 5(a) states that when someone is injured or killed by any act or omission by a criminal act of violence, in which incest and sexual assault would be included, a Board may decide to award compensation to the victim or the person responsible for their care. A survivor is required to ask for compensation within a year of the assault, but the Board can extend this period if they think it is warranted. Compensation can be given for expenses directly linked to the injury or death, financial losses of the survivor if the assault resulted in an inability to work, financial losses of dependents if the assault resulted in the death of their provider, pain and suffering, maintenance of a child born as the result of rape and any other financial losses resulting from the assault that the Board decides is reasonable to give.

A conviction under the *Criminal Code* is considered conclusive evidence that the assault took place. However, a survivor can also ask for compensation even if he or she has never initiated any criminal charges against the attacker. The Board can award a maximum of $25,000 or periodic payments of $1,000 per month. The total amount that can be paid out to a survivor is limited to a lump sum of $150,000 or a periodic payment total of $250,000. Any money paid under this Act is not subject to garnishment or attachment orders.

Conclusion

Hopefully, the above discussion will be of some assistance to those who wish to use our legal system to seek redress for child sexual assault. There is some indication that the time limits currently set on starting a civil action will change. In the area of criminal law, I am much less optimistic. All too frequently I hear of cases where the police and/or the Crown refuse to lay charges or drop them after because the survivors are not seen as or believed to be credible. This is especially true when the complainant is a young child. Often survivors faced with police inaction feel there is nothing they can do. It is good to remember that they can initiate a criminal complaint themselves by going before a justice of the peace. This may not result in a conviction or even cooperation by the police or the Crown, but it may be worthwhile.

Keep in mind that laws may have changed since the writing of this article, and that they vary from province to province. This will hopefully give you an overview of your options, but for more accurate and up-to-date advice, please consult a lawyer or community legal service in your area.

Whatever legal route a survivor chooses to take, it is imperative that you have support. The legal system will offer you none and will often drain all your financial and emotional resources. So, if you have the resources and determination to go to court, also make sure you have a support system that will be there for you throughout the process, and remember it probably will take a long time.

Notes

1. R.S.O. 1980 c.82.
2. R.S.C. 1985 c. C-46.
3. Alan Linden, *Canadian Tort Law* (Fourth edition). Butterworths, Toronto, 1988.
4. Linden.
5. Linden.
6. For example in Manitoba and B.C. there is a two year *Limitation Period* and one year in Saskatchewan. Interestingly, offenses to property in many provinces are afforded a longer limitation period in which individuals can commence an action.
7. For example,
Limitation Act, R.S.O. 1980 c.240 s.47.
Limitation Act, R.S.B.C. 1979 c.236 s.7

Limitation of Actions Act R.S.S. 1979 c.L-15 s.6
8. *Supra,* note 7.
9. *Supra,* note 7.
10. [1989] O.J. No. 2329.
11. *Supra,* note 10.
12. *Supra,* note 10.
13. *Supra,* note 10.
14. *Supra,* note 10.
15. *Supra,* note 10.
16. B.(K.L.) v. B.(K.E.) [1991] M.J. no. 144.
17. *Constitution Act,* 1982 R.S.C. 1985 Appendix II, No.44.
18.

7. Everyone has the right to life, liberty and security of the person and the right not to be deprived thereof except in accordance with the principles of fundamental justice.

15(1) Every individual is equal before and under the law and has the right to the equal protection and benefit of the law without discrimination and, in particular, without discrimination based on race, national or ethnic origin, colour, religion, sex, age or mental or physical disability.

19. Recommendations for a New Limitations Act, *Report of the Limitations Act Consultation Group.* March, 1991.
20. [1990] O.J. No. 529.
21. [1990] O.J. No. 2181.
22. *R v. P.*(J.C.) [1989] Manitoba Court of Appeal.
23. *R. v. C.*(M.N.) [1989] Supreme Court of Newfoundland.
24. S.11 of the Charter sets out specific protection available to everyone facing proceedings in criminal and penal matters.

11. Any person charged with an offense has the right
(b) to be tried within a reasonable time.

25. [1989] O.J. No. 339

Identifying Your Own Healing Path

Clarissa Chandler

Editor's Note: This article is an edited interview by Regan McClure with Clarissa Chandler.

When I think about healing I believe the first step is to simply recognize that childhood sexual abuse has occurred and actually had an impact. Becoming aware is more than just knowing that you've been injured and taking action to heal, it's also a coming to consciousness. The first step in developing this consciousness is being willing to say "I have a feeling, I have a belief about my life that is not necessarily congruent with everything I've ever heard about who I am". As childhood sexual abuse survivors, that's our experience — knowing we have been abused but being told in some way or another that it didn't occur or didn't matter. That denial of consciousness and all that we have heard, felt, tasted and smelled means that we don't trust that first instinctive feeling that says 'something's not right'. To start on the healing path we have to be willing to risk that others don't agree. People can often go through a great deal of 'treatment' and still not have taken that first step. Everything else depends on that ability to believe and trust our own senses.

Survivors heal themselves, some with therapists and some without. We can evaluate different methods of healing by the degree to which they lead us to a greater sense of self and consciousness about what we each see, feel, hear and know. Really good therapy, which includes many diverse methods, helps develop that consciousness. What is 'good' therapy depends on the person, for some people talking about their experiences is a powerful tool and for them talk therapies would be very useful. Other people might need to be doing bodywork first, or creative therapies.

There are a couple of things to keep in mind when shopping for therapists. The first is that you look for someone who has at least a concept of sexual assault. Look for a facilitator who can give a framework, not of answers, but of possibilities. Everyone's path is different, but there are commonalities. When you have someone to initially guide you through the possibilities, it reduces your fear enough to learn more about how you are processing your experiences and healing.

For me, the key issue is not that someone works with a therapist but that the survivor has help. The isolation of sexual assault is designed to make the survivor feel alone. Finding a mentor, who may be a different person at different times, who is 'in your corner' is a really powerful process. We need someone to be on our side and take the time to find out what's going on. Basic caring, comfort and loving is really profound. We tend to underestimate the value of friendship. I don't just mean hang-out buddies, but someone who is willing to mentor and support development. They don't need to have solutions but will work with you as part of a team to find them. As survivors we tend to frame the world by thinking that "anything that needs to get done we better do ourselves" because that's what it took to survive. That served us really well, but we tend to minimize the fact that people who don't have support don't do as well as people who have resources. That's one of the reasons that people in the mainstream tend to do better than people on the fringe — because they have more access to people, places and things around them which can give them support and resources.

We often minimize the stress and heroic efforts we put into surviving by ourselves because we succeeded and it becomes daily life for us. When help is available we see it as a point of vulnerability rather than a source of strength. You should be able to go to someone and say "I can't take it". We could do it alone, but it will consume much more of our life than if we have help. Why sacrifice our body, our play, our energy, our spirit or our fun to get through this alone? A lot of people pitched in with the dirt, someone should be here supporting us in the healing.

The more people who talk about sexual assault, the more the issue reaches general awareness. It can help to go to support groups, write in your journal, read about other's stories, but it's also important to have flesh and blood contact of someone on your side so you can afford to look at what's wrong. If you don't feel you can afford to take time out, you'll be afraid you'll get distracted from bare survival and falter. With another person, with help, you can take the time to be replenished.

I think it's important to acknowledge the losses as well as the gains of the healing process. The grief we have to go through brings us to a deeper level of consciousness about our experiences and ourselves. You're not healing 'wrong' if it seems painful — the healing process shouldn't be sold to people as nothing but happiness or pain. It involves a lot of joy, and also pain and hard work. It's good to know that from the beginning.

Figure out where to go for replenishment. For some people it's a real spiritual awakening, for others the actual abuse took place in that context and they need to seek out a very secular resource. Trying to get help from the mental health care system has proven to be so dangerous and damaging to some that they need to seek out another type of resource. These resources don't have to be restricted but all of them — whether the mental health system, a church, self-help etc. — need to be taken with caution. The person or resource you choose has to be on your side, willing to hear the truth about your life and willing to take the journey with you to find out what the next step is. That may turn out to be your neighbour, minister, therapist, friend or a support group. Look for someone who can be there for you across time.

'Sexual assault survivor' is not a diagnosis. We don't need to be 'fixed'. If you suffered profound abuses but were able to fight back or had people to believe you, it shifts what you believe about yourself and the world. The different coping strategies that were available to us means that we could protect ourselves in some ways and not in others. We want a mentor to assist us in finding out what the similarities are in our experiences of abuse and its impact, as well acknowledge the uniqueness of our experiences.

Along with mentorship, we need physical resources to help us heal. The bottom line is that we all live in a body. What gives us humanity is living in a human body. Our first and most valued resource is our body. Even when the sexual abuse took the form of a non-touching type of assault, it still conveys to us that 'my body is not mine, it can be owned and used for somebody else's benefit without my consent'. That communication to a child is devastating because in order to maintain control we have to divorce ourselves from our bodies in some way. Once we come to consciousness about our abuse, and that our experience of it is important and real, we also need to know that the abuse happened in a body. Our bodies may now have pains and memories; they need to speak as well as our voices. The felt knowledge needs to be expressed as much as the intellectual awareness — whether through dance, mime, exercise, bodywork or massage.

Claiming one's body, integrating it and determining what happens to it is essential. Often the abuse takes us to two extremes, one is an almost religious attention to our physical well-being, the other is a total lack of interest. Long-term victimization, in which we must include the period of silencing and shaming, means that we have taken a sustained hit to our bodies, psyches and spirits. We are stressed to the limit, and we need to replenish our energy and vitality. In the busyness of surviving we forget about resting and keep a defensive posture in our lives. We don't take the time to take care of ourselves. It's a common thing to see survivors switch from religiously avoiding to religiously doing. We still get no respite, no peace, no port in the storm. We have to learn, sometimes for the first time, to feel comfortable in our bodies, find tranquillity, be able to sleep, rest and get up, eat and be satisfied, be held and comforted. The focus is often 'what do I need to protect, defend or go after?'. I tend not to use the word crisis to describe this state, but 'sustained stress' or distress. Within the long periods of stress there are also crises. It's like living in a war zone, sometimes the bombs fall and then you go back to the stress of pacing and waiting. The idea of respite means to get out of the war zone. We may go after the right therapist, line up the right support group and aggressively attack our healing and recovery, but it won't feel right. All of the right pieces are there but we still haven't learned to trust our instincts. We continue to believe that all the support is temporary so we have to use it all now or it won't be enough. I've seen survivors aggressively seek the healing as aggressively as they sought to protect themselves, and find little peace because there was no respite.

For lesbians and gay men, we feel there is little respite because there's a lot out there that says we shouldn't be alive. That added oppression reinforces the idea that that's how life should be anyway. I find it really important when dealing with childhood sexual assault survivors to also deal with homophobia and racism at the same time. Homophobia and racism affect the quality of life for us as individuals as well as our communities. If we feel that oppression is our only option and just trying to survive it is our only life posture, it breeds a level of callousness toward each other. However, we really need each other to survive. We have a lot of casualties. If we accept victimization as a reasonable life experience, there's no room to go beyond survival to healing. The experiences of assault and healing goes hand in hand with issues around healing from the impact of racism. The goal of all oppression is to persuade people that they do not have the right to their own resources or themselves. For example, the abuser persuading the child s/he should sacrifice his/her body for the perpetrator's pleasure, that Black people should work harder and benefit less, that lesbians and gay men should not appear publicly. Oppression determines who gets discarded and who gets protected. It's essential to face the reality that racism has created barriers and hurdles for people of colour in the healing process. Acknowledging this in the midst of the pain adds some reality to the magnitude of the struggle.

It isn't a coincidence that people who have the resources and the access get better faster than people without. Added oppression compounds the damage and complicates healing. Communities need healing to complete the process of personal healing. Personal healing facilitates community healing; it's a cyclical and rhythmic process.

The urge to be silent about our experiences, is reinforced by a lot of myths we have about children; that they don't remember, they grow out of pain, they somehow aren't real or their feelings don't count. As adults, we are also encouraged to forget our childhood emotions and experiences. Opening ourselves up to those emotional experiences is really an exercise in being terrified.

We also have to deal with the myth that sexual abuse creates gays and lesbians. It makes us afraid to even say those two things in the same breath. To say "I'm a lesbian and a survivor" takes a lot out of you, and you still have to face the reaction that our sexuality is part of our injury, or perhaps that we were abused because we were lesbians or gay men. To say that "I'm a lesbian and a survivor and I'm Black" means that you face the response "I just knew it — it's those Black people abusing each other and creating all those gays and lesbians". The power of those myths to ostracize and silence us makes it hard for us to feel good about our sexuality. We need to make connections about how these things interact and affect how we've experienced the world, but not in this pathological way.

I've worked with hundreds of survivors, both women and men, lesbian, gay and straight, and I've found that what has been most affected is not sexual orientation, but sexual expression. This is one of the realities that makes it even more painful to heal. We must already overcome so much to acknowledge our sexuality and our experiences of abuse; to add the fact that we have trouble feeling or expressing our sexual desires often makes the struggle seem futile. When the world views you as only being sexual, having problems with your sexual expression seems like a cruel joke. It's a source of humiliation to admit that all these things are true at once. It makes it confusing for a lesbian or gay man to say "I'm having sexual problems" to anyone, because then people will think that you're really straight, rather than recognizing that the issue is in expressing the feeling. We don't have the emotional and psychological resources to express our desires because of the devastation of sexual abuse.

Part of the healing journey is being able to see what was previously unknown. If we let ourselves be confused over issues like 'does my sexual inhibition mean I'm really just straight?', it prevents us from paying attention to what our desires are and then acting upon them to get what we want. There are many levels of self-awareness; that I have a right to be who I am rather than what others expect me to be, that I have a right to want whatever I want rather than what others think I should want and that I have a right to pursue my happiness rather than live my life according to the expectations of others. All of these levels of coming to consciousness are a part of healing.

Learning to give ourselves daily kindnesses and having self-compassion is essential. Having to survive on instinct and gut reaction for so long, it's nice to be able to stop and look around and say "I think I might like that" or "I'm going to try this now". Becoming aware of the spectrum of possibilities is very pleasant, but also confusing.

I try not to think of this journey as fixing something or making it better, it's really about healing, growing and developing. The process does involve pain, but there will be a life after that pain. Once we learn to process and move through pain, we can open ourselves up to other experiences. That path, however, can take many different directions. The main idea is to let the pain pass through us and not lodge in us. Affirm that this is my life and I'm living it. I'm not giving it away, sacrificing it or pretending it's not here — I'm living it. I want to let it all pass through me.

The grieving, that heart pain of sadness and anger that goes with tremendous loss, is part of the process of acknowledging that I've been hit, what's the damage, what resources do I need and how can I create new choices for myself? It's okay to stop in the midst of this sorting out process and scream, vent, talk and express about things for a while. By doing that, we create room for joy. If something is new and different, it's alarming — whatever the sensation. We had burdens placed on us as children; if they're suddenly lifted, it's very alarming. I think it's really helpful to name it as joy, tolerate it, figure out that you won't float away, and then try to find out what kind of activities consume the joyful person — because that begins the whole quest of 'what do I like, what do I want?'. It's a journey that can take us back to sadness when you may realize that you've organized your whole life around something you never wanted.

The journey into healing often branches out into other aspects of our lives. Often, we start with the quest to make our lives better as survivors of childhood sexual abuse, but across time it becomes just the question of 'how can I make my life fit me better?'. That periodically involves looking at the abuse again in a new light, but it doesn't remain forever and always the healing path of sexual abuse. It becomes the healing path of creating life the way you want it. Surviving is just one of the pieces in the picture.

"Why me?" is a question that needs to be answered. There's usually a whole lot of answers, but we have to ask them before we can get to the bottom line; that it was me, is me, and I can either let the abuse live in me or I can work and use it to live my life. It can bring us to consciousness about how non-random certain events are in our lives. Knowing that race, class, sexual orientation, gender and age have affected our experiences can help us acknowledge the political realities that exist in our lives. Our healing is affected by those realities.

Realizing that my political position is relatively precarious means that I can then acknowledge my need for additional resources, rather than thinking "Why isn't therapy alone good enough for me when it's fine for someone else?" It became more important for me to do my healing in multiple contexts with women, lesbians, Black women and men, people of colour and other contexts of my experience that I needed to work through. Being treated and treated and not getting better can be explained with a small dose of reality — some people don't want me to do well, in fact they really object to my existence. I need to know that and protect myself if I want to heal myself.

The healing journey, in my mind, isn't complete with just talking about activities and changes in personal consciousness. As communities, it's important for us to make room and create institutions that acknowledge this reality. We also need use the resources from straight communities and make them accountable to us. For some of us, it's a mental health issue, and if we want to use the mental health system it should be safe and accessible to us. Within our communities, we need to have all of ourselves there in order to be healthy, we shouldn't have to leave a part of ourselves at the door. Sexual abuse is a part of our lives and experiences, acknowledging that doesn't have to minimize a positive sense of lesbian and gay pride. Speaking this truth doesn't bring a lie to our positive sense of self. It's also about other survivors, listening to them, learning that my own experience isn't the only sexual abuse experience ever learned, the camaraderie and comfort from understanding that there are commonalities between experiences, even though they're not the same. This joining is very powerful.

Contributors' Notes

Carol Allen is a lesbian feminist law student at Queen's University. She is committed to making law more accessible and accountable, especially to those who are often more abused than protected by our legal justice system.

Laura Ardiel is a white able-bodied 31 year old lesbian of mainly Irish and English descent. "Writing is one of my major healing tools."

Karen Augustine is a writer and mixed media artist living in Toronto. She's had worked published in the Sister Vision anthology *Piece of My Heart*.

Becca* was in the nursing profession for 24 years and burnt out in 1986. Presently she is in her final year of undergraduate studies in Sociology and Women's Studies. "Much time has been spent in individual and group therapy, along with therapeutic massage, in order to overcome the pain and anger resulting from my abuse and I feel fortunate to say that these processes have helped enormously."

Lorna Boschman is a media artist who lives and works in Vancouver. Her work reveals subjects that are generally hidden from view. In addition to production work, she also teaches classes. Two of her videos are part of the National Gallery's Permanent Collection in Ottawa.

Inga-Britt* is a 22 year old lesbian and survivor of incest, who loves men just as much as women. At 19 she left home, Germany, to Toronto. The past three years have been marked with transition and transformation. She does work in the recovery field in several ways. "To my friends who also chose to walk the path of healing, I am thankful for your determination, strength, inspiration and power."

Valerie Cain is 39 years old, born in Hamilton, Ontario. She is now settled and settling in Roberts Creek, B.C. and her life is becoming easier. "This place has become home, friends have become family, and my family (now that they know me) are becoming friends."

Clarissa Chandler is a facilitator, organizer, writer and counsellor with over ten years of experience working with childhood sexual assault survivors. "I am experienced at healing and claiming my life for myself in the context of being a Black lesbian having come to terms with childhood sexual assault and physical abuse."

Charles* is twenty something, and continues to struggle with his emotional honesty. He has many large creative dreams for his life, and although at times his life is difficult, "there is much more vitality since I have begun to heal some old wounds. Only now am I beginning to believe that I am deserving of a passionate healthy relationship."

Steven Gauvin is presently residing in British Columbia, studying psychology. He is majoring in Arts and Education. Steven intends to counsel street kids and students at post-secondary level. "I am a survivor, not a victim. Perhaps together, we all can offer more hope for the future."

Andrew Griffin was born and raised on Prince Edward Island. He is currently raging festive in Ottawa where he makes a living as a journalist and editor. He is also working as a member of Gay and Lesbian Ottawa Writers (GLOW).

Rick Hammond* is a media monitor, writer and broadcaster, who attended the University of Ottawa and Algonquin College.

His articles have appeared in *New Federation Magazine, The Ottawa Citizen, Sightlines* and *Metro,* among others. His screenplay, "The Whale of Desire" was made into a short documentary film earlier this year. He lives in Toronto.

Rhonda Hackett is a lesbian of African descent, a writer, traveller, counsellor and a committed community activist. She is on a personal journey to affirm her emotional needs.

Richard Hofmann was born and raised in Calgary, Alberta. He started writing at the age of 16 to deal with the emotional and sexual abuse. "Since my diagnosis as HIV positive in 1983, I have centered most my energies on keeping healthy and writing."

David John* is 29 and intends to remain that way. This is his second published article in 10 years, but plans to write a bit more regularly. "I owe a lot of people letters."

Sophia Kelly* is a 22 year old lesbian witch, who lives in Vancouver, B.C. She sings, writes, talks, heals and actively supports herself and other survivors in her community.

Louise Karch is an Outward Bound instructor and a student at OISE. "Special thanks go to Professor Kathy Rockhill and Outward Bound's women of courage."

Valerie Laub is an actor, writer, clown and fa-silly-tator of play therapy workshops for adults. Having finally learned to breathe both underwater and rare air, she is now discovering the lush oxygen of life on Earth.

Z. Love* has recently moved to Toronto. This is her first story in print and she would like to have more things published. "This story is dedicated to Lisa."

Regan McClure is a white, middle-class, able-bodied lesbian. She is currently living with her lover, would like to have a cat and works way too much as a member of the Queer Press collective.

ki namaste is a graduate student in semiotics at l'Universite du Quebec in Montreal. His work focusses on gender and identity within queer punk cultural representations. He's still trying to figure out if he's a fag, a lipstick lesbian, or some as-yet unnamed social mutant.

Jean Noble was born into a white, working class family in Kingston, Ontario and after many years (and much discombolution) has finally situated herself in Edmonton, Alberta, where she is about to (among other things) finish her B.A. in English at the University of Alberta. She has discovered a new circle of 'playmates' and a very fine therapist to whom she send much love and thanx (hunka, hunka). "I live alone with my computer, leather jacket and mountain bike, and I spend my spare time napping."

John David Pastway is a writer. He was born in Barry's Bay, Thanksgiving Day, 1961. He has lived throughout northern and southern Ontario. He has been strongly influenced by Emily Dickinson, Sylvia Plath and e.e. cummings. He graduated from Wilfid Laurier with a B.A. in English Lit and Film Theory. His poems have been in *WLU Poetry, N.A.R.C., Rites* and *Toronto Life.*

Whyte Ravyn* is a writer who is just coming together. She would like to thank the unseen warrior, the storyteller, the children and the rest of the cast of thousands for their courage, voices and sacrifices.

Sapphire* is a Black American poet, novelist, short story writer and performance artist. Her work has appeared in numerous anthologies and journals in the United States and

England. The author of a self-published book of poetry, *Meditations on the Rainbow,* she is currently compiling a collection of prose and poetry.

Stefan is from Nova Scotia. He tested HIV positive in May 1982, and is currently an active board member of the Black Coalition for AIDS Prevention (BlackCAP) and various other AIDS organizations. His experiences are in buddying, AIDS outreach, AIDS education, AIDS prevention and public speaking. Stefan is 6′1", weighs 205 lbs., likes to frolic and seeks same for fun, romance and adventure.

Stevi Urben writes poetry, script and lyrics, when she listens to herself. "A friend came up to me and said, 'Have you got a moment? I want an answer to all the unexplainable things in life!' I said, 'I don't have any answers, I can only hope to live through them!'."

Charlene Williams* likes tattoos & beaches. Fembutch. She grew up in Toronto, has lived in Vancouver for nine years. She has been sober for one year and dares to dream new dreams.

*Asterisks indicate that the author has used a pseudonym.